THIS BRAIN HAD A MOUTH

THIS BRAIN HAD A MOUTH

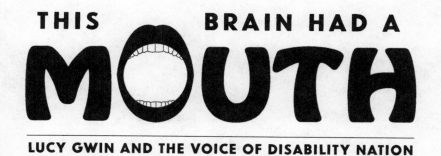

LUCY GWIN AND THE VOICE OF DISABILITY NATION

JAMES M. ODATO

*To John,
who knows a good
story when he sees it.*

Jim Odato

UNIVERSITY OF MASSACHUSETTS PRESS
AMHERST AND BOSTON

A portion of Part One copyright © 2019 by James M. Odato

Foreword, Acknowledgments, Prologue, Parts Two-Five,
and Epilogue © 2021 by University of Massachusetts Press
All rights reserved
Printed in the United States of America

ISBN 978-1-62534-619-3 (paper); 618-6 (hardcover)

Designed by Deste Roosa
Set in Cormorant Garamond and Newcastle
Printed and bound by Books International, Inc.

Cover design by Kristina Kachele Design, llc
Cover photo © Alan Farkas.

Library of Congress Cataloging-in-Publication Data
Names: Odato, James M., author.
Title: This brain had a mouth : Lucy Gwin and the voice of disability
nation / James M. Odato.
Description: Amherst : University of Massachusetts Press, [2021] | Includes
bibliographical references and index.
Identifiers: LCCN 2021017176 (print) | LCCN 2021017177 (ebook) | ISBN
9781625346186 (hardcover) | ISBN 9781625346193 (paperback) | ISBN
9781613768945 (ebook) | ISBN 9781613768952 (ebook)
Subjects: LCSH: Gwin, Lucy. | Women social reformers—United
States—Biography. | People with disabilities—United States—Biography.
Classification: LCC HV28.G88 O43 2021 (print) | LCC HV28.G88 (ebook) |
DDC 362.4092 [B]—dc23
LC record available at https://lccn.loc.gov/2021017176
LC ebook record available at https://lccn.loc.gov/2021017177

British Library Cataloguing-in-Publication Data
A catalog record for this book is available from the British Library.

CONTENTS

FOREWORD

NADINA LASPINA

Nadina LaSpina is a disability rights activist, teacher, and author of the memoir Such a Pretty Girl: A Story of Struggle, Empowerment, and Disability Pride. *Active in the disability rights movement for forty years, she has worked with groups that include Disabled in Action and ADAPT. She was a longtime friend and colleague of Lucy Gwin.*

I had been reading the manuscript of the book now in your hands, in which Lucy Gwin, editor and publisher of *Mouth* magazine, comes alive through author James Odato's expertise with words, when, while crossing a street in my wheelchair, I got hit by a car. In the hospital, saying things that made no sense, afraid and emotional, my surroundings seeming even more alien because of double vision, I identified with Lucy. I felt even closer to her when the hospital's social worker casually mentioned that, since I had no one at home to take care of me, they would transfer me to a rehabilitation center. "Just for a couple of weeks," she said. Oh yeah? I knew that if I lost my cool, like Lucy—a volcano constantly on the verge of eruption—I might end up for who knows how long in a "rehab" facility, which for many of us in Disability Nation could be the equivalent of a nursing home. My fear worked like magic. Suddenly I became coherent and regained my powers of persuasion. I convinced the doctors that they should send me home.

My injury, unlike Lucy's, was only a complicated concussion with no lasting damage to my brain.

Lucy's brain injury marked her introduction to Disability Nation. Odato tells us in vivid detail how, for free-spirited, fiery Lucy, the loss of freedom and the abuse, her own and what she witnessed happening to others, was unbearable, a story of her "captivity" that we all heard upon meeting her.

She launched her magazine in 1990, around the time of the Americans with Disabilities Act.

The disability rights movement at that point had been in existence for years. How many? That depends on who's telling the story.

Historians cite early occurrences such as the first school for deaf students, the invention of Braille, the publication of Helen Keller's autobiography . . . all important moments in our history, of course, but certainly not marking the beginning of a new movement. Also listed are "charities" with the goal of funding a "cure"—money raised in ways that we later found offensive and harmful, such as "telethons," which turned us into objects of pity, and against which our movement organized many protests. They were "for us" and not "by us." Some got it right, such as the National Association of the Deaf, founded in 1880 as an organization run by deaf people against "oralism," and the National Federation of the Blind, founded in 1940 by Jacobus tenBroek, who was blind.[1]

In New York City, my home, we like to brag about an early instance of rebellion by the short-lived (1935–1938) League of the Physically Handicapped. League members twice rode by flatbed truck to Washington, DC, to protest the exclusion of the physically disabled from President Franklin Delano Roosevelt's Works Progress Administration program. Many in the group wore braces and used crutches—displaying their paralysis, courtesy of polio, at a time when FDR was hiding his own.

So, when/how/by whom was our movement started? No one single person starts a social movement. There may be one individual who serves as the spark. Many of us who became part of the disability rights movement had been involved or influenced by the great civil rights, feminist, antiwar, and gay rights movements of the sixties and seventies. As a teen, I had dreamed of being a Freedom Rider—no matter that I couldn't get on a bus, and was undergoing surgeries, having had polio as an infant in Italy; as a young woman, I'd gone in my wheelchair to many protests against the Vietnam War; and I proudly called myself a feminist. There were certainly plenty of people with disabilities ready to rise up. Medical advances and technology had made it easier for us to survive and to find one another. In hospitals, in special schools, in summer camps,[2] we compared notes. We agreed we had had enough of being treated like second-class citizens because of our disabilities.

On the West Coast, the spark was Ed Roberts, a polio quadriplegic who slept in an iron lung. He insisted on attending the University of California at Berkeley, which was becoming a hotbed of student activism.

Odato tells us that Lucy's interview with Ed Roberts was the beginning of a great friendship. Ed Roberts redefined "independence," as the control people with disabilities have over their own lives. Independence was measured, not by the tasks one could perform without assistance—which was the goal of rehabilitation—but by the life one could have with all the needed services and supports.[3]

In New York City, the "spark" was Judy Heumann, who sued when the Board of Education denied her a license to teach because, also as a result of polio, she used a wheelchair. It was 1970. That same year, she started Disabled in Action, known as the first cross-disability civil rights organization.

In 1968, at the University of Tulsa in Oklahoma, Lex Frieden, quadriplegic as a result of a car accident, founded what would become Win Independence Now. Odato tells us that Frieden taught Lucy a lot about our movement. Frieden later worked with Justin Dart Jr. helping to draft the Americans with Disabilities Act.

As early as 1961, Fred Fay made his mark after becoming spinal cord injured as a teenager. He co-founded Opening Doors in Washington, DC, and went on to attend the University of Illinois at Urbana-Champaign, the first wheelchair-accessible university in the United States, thanks to early advocacy by students.[4] In 1974 Fay founded the Boston Center for Independent Living and became the first president of the American Coalition of Citizens with Disabilities.[5]

An account of all that happened in the twenty years before our Lucy burst onto the scene would take way too many pages. We advocated and got laws passed, such as the Education for All Handicapped Children Act, later to become the Individuals with Disabilities Education Act (IDEA); we fought for access of many forms; we started centers for independent living all over the country; we fought stereotypes, we talked about disability studies, we protested, we got arrested.

To get the ADA passed, our fragmented community had to come together. That happened when 180 national organizations, some having little or nothing in common with one another, endorsed the bill,[6] from charities like Easter Seals, to Act-Up, to the protest group American Disabled for Accessible Public Transit, ADAPT.

Once the ADA was law, ADAPT's issue changed from accessible public transportation to freeing people from institutions—going back to its origin, the freeing by ADAPT co-founder Wade Blank of people with disabilities from a nursing home. The acronym came to stand for American Disabled for Attendant Programs Today. The stick figure in the wheelchair breaking chains became our icon, and "Free Our People" was our battle cry.

Lucy joined our movement at the right time for her, and it was the right time for our movement as well. We needed Lucy just as much as she needed us. The coming together of our community in the fight for the ADA had been a bit forced. The young activists who criticize us today are right. In the beginning, the leaders were predominantly those with physical disabilities, white, and well educated.

Lucy recognized the lack of diversity in our movement. She saw the importance of inclusion.

Groups representing people with different disabilities tended to remain separate. In 1993, the man who would become my husband, Daniel Robert, and I organized the Disability Independence Day March.[7] Our biggest challenge was getting everyone from deaf people to psychiatric survivors to individuals with intellectual disabilities to participate.

People with physical disabilities usually are encouraged and praised by family and friends for compensating for our "defective" bodies with our sharp minds. Many people without disabilities assume that any physical disability also affects the brain: some brilliant people with cerebral palsy and other disabilities that may affect speech were judged "ineducable." As the great Ed Roberts, in his early days of advocacy, said, "I'm only paralyzed from the neck down, not from the neck up."[8]

We definitely owe Lucy an enormous debt for bringing to the fore-front of the movement those of us whose disability is not just from the neck down.

When Lucy joined the movement, the first commercials were appearing on TV showing wheelchair users, usually white and male, ath-letes, or business types with their suits and briefcases. People without disabilities wanted to think of us as being just like them. Some in disability nation fell into that trap, buying in to the elusive pursuit of normalcy. Not Lucy. She had never been like everyone else, or like anyone else. Reading this book, I realized that was true even before her accident.

At the time, our movement was going into a more serious and more "tame" mode—with activists getting political appointments; disability studies trying to be recognized as a new field in universities; centers for independent living, afraid of losing their government funding, turning from hotbeds of activism to provider agencies. We needed Lucy to keep the passion and excitement of true activism alive, with her subjective brand of journalism, her shameless agitator articles, her consumer reports on the CILs.

ADAPT was really on the outskirts then, accused of harming the movement with its wild, outrageous tactics. Even Mary Johnson, editor of the wonderful *Disability Rag*, which preceded *Mouth*, criticized the "undignified" crawl up the Capitol steps that ADAPT organized prior to the ADA's passage. Not Lucy. Because she herself had been "in captivity," she would do anything to "free our people." She understood and loved ADAPT. And Lucy never loved in the abstract; she loved us as a group and as individuals. She was truly one of us. So, at actions, she hung out, got drunk, argued and fought, fell in love, had sex, and got her heart broken. Odato describes it all in detail. In the eighteen years it managed to survive, *Mouth*—through Lucy's words and Tom Olin's photos—made ADAPT a household word in Disability Nation.

Lucy proved herself to be not just a writer, activist, and agitator but also an amazing organizer when she took the lead and worked tirelessly on the Not Dead Yet action in front of the US Supreme Court on January 8, 1997.[9] Not Dead Yet, founded by Diane Coleman in 1996 to give voice to the disability rights opposition to legalizing assisted suicide and euthanasia, is still going strong.[10] Lucy was haunted by the thought that most people without disabilities thought disability a fate worse than death. Odato describes the action in detail, mentioning my name as one of the people Lucy welcomes and hugs at the very successful rally. No hug ever felt so good to me. I was exhausted—our buses had left for Washington at two a.m.—and freezing cold.

I read *Mouth* because I needed a shot in the arm of Lucy's energy. Since *Mouth*'s last issue, and since Lucy died, there have been some changes in the disability movement. In recent years, activism has been mostly online, which makes connecting easier and faster. Our young activists speak of "disability justice" rather than "disability rights." Rather than equal rights and equal opportunities, this "new wave" talks about how ableism relates to other forms of oppression, racism, Christian supremacy, sexism, xenophobia, queer-and-transphobia . . . and how all forms of oppression are intertwined. The words most often used today are "intersectional" and "interdependence."

Young activists write about their dreams of a world where there is no more oppression, where all have what they need, where the planet is safe and flourishing, and where all people/all bodies are valued, appreciated, and respected.

What would Lucy say to these newcomers to the movement? Would she think of them as naïve or would she say, "This world you're dreaming of is the kind of world I always wanted"?

ACKNOWLEDGMENTS

Lucy Gwin touched a lot of lives and left behind vivid recollections. I am grateful to more than 120 people who shared theirs. Among those who were most helpful were old friends from Rochester, New York, the so-called "tribe," some of whom first latched onto Gwin in Chicago or elsewhere in Illinois. I thank you all, especially Joe Maurer, who took me on a tour of the neighborhoods, buildings, and residences where Gwin once worked, partied, and lived and to the likely site of her biography-changing car accident; Chris Pulleyn, who pulled together loose threads with keen insight; and Fred Spears, who knew Gwin's family in Indianapolis and was with her during important moments of her life. Others who helped me collect key information include Lee London, David Skates, Peter Walker, Nancy Fairless, and Sue Dawson. One friend preferred anonymity, but thank you nevertheless for allowing me to use your valuable backup for Gwin's story of her breakout from the rehab facility.

From the disability rights movement, many provided insights. Topping the list was photographer Tom Olin, perhaps the most generous spirit who ever entered Gwin's orbit. Activist and leader Kathleen Kleinmann, who shouldered many responsibilities for Gwin during her lifetime and after her death, provided material that was priceless. She opened the door for me to a storeroom of documents that might have gone to the landfill if not for her foresight. Mike Oxford and Kevin Siek in Topeka added significant material, as did Yoshiko Dart in Washington, DC. Others were important sources as well: Josie Byzek, Janine Bertram Kemp, Teresa Torres, and Jennifer Burnett chief among them, as well as cartoonist Scott H. Chambers and former staffers Bruce Faw and Joe Ehman.

Three outstanding English instructors at the University at Albany assisted in many ways. Distinguished Professor Ronald A. Bosco, an accomplished biographer in his own right, provided enormous support. Professor Jeffrey Berman, a memoirist with a deep sensitivity to issues involving death, read early chapters with care. Professor Laura Wilder, a wordsmith and author, offered smart and commonsensical ideas. My wife, Teresa Buckley, a keen editor, helped firm up sentences.

ACKNOWLEDGMENTS

I applaud, of course, the University of Massachusetts, especially Robert Cox, the head of special collections and university archives, who acted on historian Fred Pelka's recommendation to gather Gwin's papers for public use. Kudos to Pelka and the Bancroft Library at the University of California at Berkeley for housing Pelka's oral history tapes of Gwin. I am grateful to the Rochester Public Library and Rochester city historian Christine L. Ridarsky. Always I was concerned about Gwin's family, particularly her two daughters. I appreciate the kindness of Tracy Hanes, who provided photos and facts.

Thank you to editor in chief Matt Becker, copy editor Amanda Heller, and production editor Rachael DeShano and their colleagues at the University of Massachusetts Press.

THIS BRAIN HAD A MOUTH

PROLOGUE

April 11, 2019, was a clear, sunny seventy-degree day in downtown Pittsburgh. On the sidewalk across the street from an artists' exhibit space, a group of people in wheelchairs waited. They had ridden to the Iron City in a van from the independent living center in nearby Washington, Pennsylvania.

These people were early for a photography show called "Road to Freedom." They chatted in the sunshine while waiting. Sixty-six-year-old Kathryn "Kate" Blaker stood out with her strawberry blond hair and a yellow-green sweater. A full-time skills trainer at the independent living center for twenty-one years, she had recently cut back her hours when walking became impossible. Blaker was eager to see the exhibit.

She contributed to the buzz of anticipation before the doors opened on photojournalist Tom Olin's presentation of disability rights activism photos. The images reflected his decades of documenting the movement in black and white, much of that time as a partner with editor and writer Lucy Gwin in the production of *Mouth* magazine, also known as "the voice of the disability nation." The wait gave Blaker time to discuss Gwin and her magazine.

Blaker had been a *Mouth* subscriber and had lived near Gwin. "It gave a different way of looking at people with disability," Blaker said. "It gave me hope." That hope, she said, centered on being seen someday "as a person and not someone with a disability." She spoke in a halting manner, squeezing out words. Her paralyzed right arm rested on her wheelchair. Her left hand clutched the air and helped her emphasize thoughts. "People saw it as an opportunity to voice their experiences," Blaker said. "At the time, there was no other way to do that."[1]

Blaker's assessment was one that numerous others in many states would make in interviews over a period of months as they too recalled *Mouth* and its creator. Founded by Gwin in Rochester, New York, in 1990, the magazine lasted eighteen years. The headquarters moved with Gwin twice, once to Topeka, Kansas, so that Gwin and Olin could be near a center for independent living and its director, Mike Oxford, whom they admired. It moved for the last time to Washington, Pennsylvania, again so Gwin could be near a center she valued and close to its longtime director,

Kathleen Kleinmann. The activist was a steady supporter of Gwin and her advocacy journalism and of Olin and his camerawork.

A good deal of the story about Lucy Gwin is laid out in files I'd found ten months earlier in my search for a great untold story. That day in spring 2018 proved to be worth the trip to the twenty-fifth floor of the W. E. B. Du Bois Library at the University of Massachusetts.

Gwin's papers there include some of her journals, letters, calendars, poetry, song lyrics, legal documents, manuscripts, and notes. Plus, the collection holds every issue of her magazine. She was intriguing, an original, a strong storyteller with a legacy as a fighter, a feminist, and a leader in her field. Moreover, she overcame substantial obstacles, some of them self-created, but including a serious head injury.

When Blaker thought about Gwin, her face brightened. She'd visited Gwin's apartment and had met her pet ferrets, too. "I liked Lucy. I did," she said. "We lost her too soon. But she did a lot with her life." She'd admired Gwin's determination to break through gender barriers, such as when Gwin became a deckhand on a boat. Blaker enjoyed hearing about Gwin's adventures. "It made a big impression on me."

Because of her cerebral palsy, Blaker at times felt underestimated, looked down on, and Gwin had experienced that too. Gwin didn't make her feel that way, Blaker said. Gwin had been dead almost five years as Blaker shared her recollections. She remembered borrowing and reading a copy of Gwin's memoir, *Going Overboard*. "I couldn't put it down."

For Blaker and others who met her, Gwin was hard to forget. Her memoir captured pieces of the spirited woman before she became a major force in the disability rights community. It arrived seven years before the life-altering accident that triggered her activism. Indeed, the rest of the story of this fierce spirit is also difficult to put down.

PART ONE

Without deviation from the norm, progress is not possible.
—*Frank Zappa*

1

Personal Ad

Everything once, nothing twice.
Loving woman with a perhaps
too fascinating history wants a
one-of-a-kind man with a sense of
direction and a history of his own
to tell. Statistics unimportant if
you've got heart, soul, and guts.
Object: more fun than anyone
has a right to expect. Drop first
name and phone to Box 5628.[1]

Wednesday, June 14, 1989, was the third day of summer rainstorms in Rochester, New York. It was also in the middle of a busy week of work and of dating for Lucy Gwin. She drove up Lake Avenue in her sporty Toyota Celica. She had a lot on her mind, including the "seven mental midgets" she had been trying to keep at bay. Those dwarfs—Hungry, Horny, Lonesome, Deceitful, Scared, Scornful, and Pissed Off to the Max—had been darting in and out of her life for years, sometimes running things. Just a few weeks earlier, she'd been telling her psychiatrist about wrestling with these little demons.

Never satisfied with her features, other than her hands, she'd been obsessing about her weight. She called herself fat. She had other worries racing around in her head as well. She'd been thinking a lot about her eccentric family. That made her feel guilty and sad. Her father, mother, and sister had all died in warm months. She pondered what month would be her last.

Her beloved mother had died just three weeks earlier in a Florida nursing home. Brain disease—Alzheimer's—had robbed Verna Gwin of her memory. She had wanted Lucy to end her suffering. Instead, Lucy had kept her imprisoned in a nursing home, something she regretted.

"Daddy," a habitual wanderer, left for good in June 1968 because of a brain tumor. His death also had not been pretty, with him raving about buried treasure. Younger sister Bridget killed herself in July 1968. She died in a Chicago hospital after landing on her skull in a plunge from a third-floor apartment. Three head cases, Lucy Gwin thought, three dead Gwins: "Brain karma."[2]

Somehow she had made it to age forty-six. She sometimes wondered how, given her past—carrying on with drugs and alcohol and a series of troubled, addicted, or violent lovers. Plus, she was hounded by those seven mental midgets. She had complained to her shrink that her life lacked a purpose, a direction.

But on this early summer night, she had a set path. It led to connecting with a man, a fellow she hardly knew named Murray. She was driving to meet him for a second date. Her career as an ad writer had come in handy in her quest to grab the attention of guys like Murray.

Personal Ad

I still won't eat my spinach. Over-30 woman with soul of a nine- year-old wants a playmate of a man. Gotta be way beyond average, single, outspoken, a part-time misfit capable of love and intense foolishness. Send proof of the last mentioned with your name and phone to Box 5914.[3]

Many of the men who had answered her personal ads in *City Newspaper*, an alternative weekly, weren't worthy of a first date in Lucy Gwin's book. Murray had passed muster. For this second time out, he had invited Gwin to dinner at his place. He had even said Gwin could bring Digger, her terrier mutt with one blue and one brown eye. The dog sat in the back seat of the Celica as Gwin waited at a stoplight and double-checked

Murray's address. She wasn't far from his house, just a left turn across the busy thoroughfare onto Birr Street.

Gwin's car was pointed uphill when it was walloped by a driver coming from the opposite direction. The downhill driver's car smashed in the front end of Gwin's Toyota. Though she had buckled her seatbelt, Gwin was thrown about the interior. Her head struck several surfaces, including the post between the windshield and the passenger side window.

Bystanders reported she was convulsing when the ambulance arrived.[4] Responders rushed her to Rochester General Hospital and rolled her into the emergency room and then to the surgery intensive care unit. Lucy Gwin had joined disability nation.[5]

2

Gwin was not a model patient. In the ER "she was alert and awake and screaming inappropriately with no active bleeding sites."[1]

Doctors determined that patient 64-55-39 did not require general surgery. They diagnosed her injury as subarachnoid hemorrhage—trauma to the right and left brain lobes. In the blurry days and nights of her hospitalization, Gwin displayed signs of brain injury. She demanded immediate gratification, expressed distress, and struck or attempted to strike nurses, staff, and aides. She was restless. She got out of bed despite four-point restraints. She needed several days of one-on-one nursing for her own protection. "Patient needs constant supervision," a nurse reported. "Pt. is very agitated . . . verbally/physically abusive at times. Other times she is tearful and emotional. She states she wants to go where she can get help," a hospital social worker wrote.[2]

Some friends visited. Her younger daughter, Christine, whom she had seen once in ten years, arrived from out of state. Neither of Gwin's ex-husbands showed up. Nor did her third husband, to whom she was still married. They had lived together for only five months after their 1983 marriage before separating. Gwin was tapping his insurance plan to cover medical bills.[3] She was angry, acted paranoid, was "highly uncooperative," a friend, Joe Maurer, recalled.[4]

Her ad agency colleagues stopped in. They did not like what they saw. "She was kind of a mess; she wasn't in a coma . . . matter of fact she was out of her mind raving," said Bruce Younger, a partner in SanFilipo Younger Associates in Rochester.[5]

The accident gave the firm an opportunity to break off their business relationship, which had spanned a few years and had deteriorated with regular blowups. Gwin had become increasingly difficult to work with—often shouting at meetings with the partners—and they considered her too bossy with clients. Although they credited her for her clever approaches and creative ad schemes, she was wearing out everyone at SanFilipo Younger. They had been impressed with her ability to develop campaigns and valued the experience she brought to the firm from her advertising career in Indianapolis and Chicago during her twenties. But she had tried to push her vision on customers. She thought she knew what they needed, and she may have been right, but it wasn't what customers asked for or what they could afford. Some clients said they didn't want to deal with her. "She was very opinionated," Younger said. In the hospital, she sounded off about the firm cutting ties. She felt abandoned, unappreciated, and owed.

She could not walk. If she tried to stand, she wobbled. She needed assistance to smoke. She suffered from "acute organic brain syndrome (sudden Alzheimer's kind of thing)," Gwin wrote later.[6] The doctor in charge declared that she should make an "almost complete recovery" within six months. Since there were no family members or friends to whom to discharge her, hospital staff concluded she would be better off transferred to a trauma rehabilitation center. Her daughter supported the discharge plan.[7]

Doctors sedated her. She received doses of antipsychotic and antianxiety medications, and an ambulance was summoned. Three weeks after her accident, and forty-eight hours after Independence Day in 1989, Lucy Gwin was whisked to a head injury rehab institution more than two hours away in Cortland, New York.[8] It was operated by New Medico, at the time the largest chain of brain rehab centers in the nation.

3

Gwin was almost cognizant when she reached New Medico Community Re-Entry Systems in Cortland. About ten minutes before she arrived, an attendant in the ambulance gave her a drag off a cigarette. She could not remember her name or much else, but thanks to the tobacco, the fog thinned. She saw a big building. It seemed like a mansion. Inside, she found her voice and immediately asked a staff member for a patient rights statement. All she received was a room.[1]

Days of minimal service followed. Christine, estranged from her mother since childhood, when she was known as "Crickie," got a report from the staff that Gwin was in poor condition. But she was making progress, despite physical therapy consisting, according to Gwin, of playing the board game Trivial Pursuit and getting tips on sorting laundry.

Most of each day she sat outdoors and wrote in a journal at a picnic table with other "inmates." Their most common activity involved smoking cigarettes. She yearned for physical contact and started a romance with a young man, an affectionate head injury patient less than half her age. "I was detained there," she wrote later. "I asked every day, often in writing, to see a doctor and learn my prognosis. I asked for a quarter (so that I might call a lawyer, or my friends, or my family). All of these requests were denied."[2] She saw an ophthalmologist once. A psychiatrist spoke with her for about ten minutes.

The attitude of the staff ranged from indifferent to criminal, she said. Her roommate, a woman named Gloria, suffered from aphasia and therefore could not speak. Gwin alleged that an aide and two accomplices raped Gloria twice. Gwin was prevented from calling 911.[3] When she told higher-ups about the assaults, they responded that Gwin had been hallucinating. She was scared. But her memory was returning. She announced to staff that she wanted to go home. Such longings, they declared, were a symptom of brain injury.

Christine, who was twenty-seven, accepted the staff's evaluation that Gwin was not ready for release.[4] Before the end of that first month at New Medico, Gwin started begging visitors to rescue her. Her friend Joe Maurer declined. The next day, a former boyfriend, Frank, arrived in his new gray Nissan truck.

"I got a frantic call from her," Frank remembered twenty-nine years later. "She said she managed to get to a phone and she called me. She said she was being raped and she saw others being raped and she thought they were 'going to kill me.'" When he got to the institution, the staff wanted to know the purpose of his visit. He said he was going to take his friend Lucy Gwin home. An administrator challenged him. Frank asked if Gwin was under arrest and was told she was not. "They said, 'She's seriously ill, she has brain injury.' They said, 'She needs twenty-four-hour care' and said if I really wanted to, I could sign her out, and I would be responsible for her.

"I think I signed 'Frank Zappa.'"[5]

He got her into the truck and worried that he might be detained by authorities on the ride back to Rochester. But nothing happened. They stopped at a thruway rest area for something to eat. Gwin was amazed she remembered how to get in and out of a truck. She noted the crows nearby, she wrote in her journal a few days later.[6] She referred to Frank several times in those post-escape journals.

In a 2018 interview, Frank said he had fond memories of Gwin. He recalled her helping him find dates by writing a personal ad for him. It was effective. "That's how I met my wife," he added. "I got responses left and right." He and Gwin had a falling-out later in 1989 and they were never in touch again. "We were getting mad a lot, and neither of us knew why, exactly," Gwin wrote.[7]

4

Back with Digger in her second-floor apartment, Gwin was improving but still not right. The two-family house at 61 Brighton Street was in a neighborhood of roomy colonial and Victorian homes. A nearby section of Rochester boasted large residences lining an avenue once occupied by the Eastman family of Kodak fame. Less than a mile away was the former home of the antislavery activist Frederick Douglass, and Gwin was beginning to think about civil rights. She was unable to walk without a cane, and she fumed about her treatment by New Medico.

She busied herself with insurance claims and counseling sessions and pain management. Her recovery was taking time. She did not know if she would be permanently injured. She complained of fuzzy vision, headaches, a ringing in her ears. "I don't have any intellectual or emotional deficits," she wrote on a yellow pad a few months after her accident. She admitted she was being entirely subjective. Her state of mind, if painted by an artist, would show a landscape at dusk and a tornado with tunnels in it, she wrote. Frank had evaluated her and decided she was "the same old asshole she always was," she jotted down in her notes. She reported that the "experts" had told her she would not write again, that she was damaged. She was furious.[1]

Lucy Gwin did indeed write. She wrote lots of letters to public health officials and law enforcement agencies demanding an investigation of New Medico. She allied with the mother of a patient at the facility. A week after she was sprung from Cortland, she wrote out a mission statement—a list of "intentions." Dated August 8, 1989, it indicated she had found a purpose in life:

Bring brain injury and its aftermath to the attention of the public
Bring New Medico and the like to the attention of state and federal
    legislators and governors
Get out of advertising and do something important with my life
    (stop "surviving")
Get the other half of my pair safely in my arms
live with other people
move with the mission as it presents itself to destroy anti-human
    structures and build human ones in their place
learn to accept true human nature as it is.[2]

"She was really grateful for that accident—it gave her a life worth living," according to David Scates, a Rochester friend. She often would credit the crash with giving her a direction, he said. The two had bonded before her accident. They would meet at her apartment to drink and work on writing. "I remember her talking about how purposeless her life was not too much before the accident."[3]

5

Over the next few months, Gwin turned her anger into activism. She and Midge DeMartino, the friend with a son at New Medico, created a magazine, *This Brain Has a Mouth.* It focused on brain injury survivors and the institutions that were supposed to serve them. In it Gwin railed against scamming rehab businesses that she said were milking insurance companies. She accused these rehab firms of soaking insurers for thousands of dollars a week for patients who were housed like prisoners. In the pages of this new enterprise, Gwin showed off her advertising skills. She had excelled at packaging concepts in her years at ad firms large and small in Indianapolis, Chicago, and Rochester. She now applied that knowledge, positioning graphics around articles about head injury victims and coining phrases such as "handicaptivity" in what was her version of journalism.

The first issue of the magazine came out a year after Frank rescued her from New Medico's facility. That July–August 1990 issue debuted at a price of $2.50 and went to a small list of subscribers. Almost at the same time, in Washington, DC, President George H. W. Bush signed into law the Americans with Disabilities Act, known as the civil rights law for millions of people dealing with some form of disability, from blindness to mobility impairments. At the ADA signing ceremony, two of the leaders who had been pushing for the measure for decades, Justin Dart Jr. and Evan Kemp, flanked Bush. They would soon have roles in Gwin's new magazine, as would a photographer who documented the historic event.

The publication was billed as "The National Magazine for People with Brains." In it, Gwin masked her identity, assuming the name "Ed the Hothead." Yet the magazine's mailing address was her home. The first issue ran twenty-four pages with two full pages of cartoons. An anonymous column "by The Publisher" was augmented by a sketch that may have been Ed the Hothead, or may have been Lucy Gwin. With knitted brow and a cigarette between his lips, the figure in the sketch sits behind a standard typewriter. Before him is a desk covered with sheets of paper, some crumpled, and a full ashtray. The column, announcing a policy of no advertisers, appealed for subscribers at $10 a year.

The 1990 and 1991 issues, which came out every two months, were black-and-white publications, crude in comparison to later editions printed in color with more in-depth stories, profiles, many letters to the editor, and gripping photos and essays. Even in its early stages, the magazine had an edge and a flair for satire. Those first issues dedicated a page to spelling out a patient's bill of rights so that people could "set themselves free of forced rehab." Citing the Magna Carta, the Declaration of Independence, and a Supreme Court decision, the advisories emphasized an adult's right to freedom. They also urged that persons being held against their will should get a lawyer.

Bruce Faw, Gwin's sole assistant at the start, considered her a great boss, good at directing and nurturing. She hired Faw right out of nearby Monroe County Community College after an introduction from a friend.[1] He produced graphics and did whatever else needed doing in those dawning months, including helping Gwin up and down stairs and lifting stacks of magazines and heavy objects. Sometimes Faw managed the office.

Gwin busied herself discovering the issues affecting her new beat. She interviewed disability rights leaders in a quest to familiarize herself with the history of the movement and to build her source list. At the start "I was dumb as a rock," she admitted in a speech in 1998.[2] Disability policy expert and activist Lex Frieden, a professor of physical medicine and rehabilitation who helped draft the Americans with Disabilities Act, had several meetings with Gwin in the 1990s as she was learning the field. "When she got into the movement, she was a neophyte," he recalled. She absorbed and questioned and learned. Soon she understood the broad array of people who could be her audience, Frieden said, and expanded the spectrum by including people of color, the deaf and the blind, and psychiatric patients. He called her "uniquely articulate" and appreciated the "raw emotion" she poured into her magazine.[3]

Faw too watched her develop. "She was one of those people who ran a fine line between brilliance and lunacy," he said.[4] She was constantly on the phone, tossing back Coca-Colas, puffing on cigarettes, developing her knowledge of the brain trauma rehab industry and its victims. And she was working to push New Medico under. As she sat at the typewriter, she would have a cigarette going in an ashtray on either side of her, Faw remembered. Her style reminded him of gonzo journalist Hunter S. Thompson. She was driven and made snap decisions. Every room of Gwin's flat, except her bedroom, was dedicated to the magazine. The big front porch was a break area. That's where Gwin would commune with visiting birds, particularly crows. One day she brought home a ferret for a pet. To make extra money and save on expenses, Faw set up a marijuana-growing operation on the third floor. The pot was pretty good, he said.

One of Gwin's close friends, a handyman she called "Slammin' Sam" Baxter, lived on the first floor with his girlfriend. Many visitors from the disability community arrived at Gwin's door, so, using packing crates, Baxter built a wheelchair ramp to the house. He and his girlfriend opened their home to these out-of-towners and made coming and going easier. Gwin inserted Baxter's name as the first publisher of the magazine. The debut issue of *This Brain Has a Mouth* was sent to residents of New Medico's Cortland rehab facility under Baxter's name, and he received a letter from the facility's program director assuring him that all the "clients" had received copies in their mail and that it was read and discussed at a two-hour open forum.[5]

Such was the start of eighteen years of publishing a magazine referred to as "the world's leading public media voice" for democracy by the disability rights leader Justin Dart Jr.[6] It would tell stories, sometimes with dark humor, of people with whom Gwin identified. She opened her pages to them to foster a spirit of community. In a 2003 issue dubbed "Dirty Words," she reminded readers of a competition she'd conducted in the fall of 1992 to "name those people," writing: "Some folks call us crips, or gimps. Some of us call ourselves handicapped. The politically correct call us people with disabilities. The politically incorrect call us *those people*." A not-for-profit that helped people with disabilities gain access to computers had previously conducted a search for the right term and had come up with "people with differing abilities." Gwin challenged her readers to improve on that phrase, offering a $50 prize for a more apt name. Responses arrived and free subscriptions went to finalists: "Dem Broke Folk," "P.O.D.s—people of disability," "Fire Hazards." The grand prize winner, Gwin declared, had the right mix of wiseass, street slang potential, and fuel for cartoons: "the Dislabled."[7] Beginning in issue 71 and for the rest of its days, the masthead promoted the magazine as "The Voice of the DisLabled Nation."

6

New Medico and the friends she'd left behind at the Cortland rehab center were always on Gwin's mind. She corresponded with some of those trauma patients and mailed letters to elected leaders, government agencies, and the FBI calling for an investigation. She telephoned journalists, federal agents, and health officials. She wrote long poems about her experience and her decision to become an activist. In one, "I Used to Wonder Why Martin Luther King Junior Used Prostitutes," Gwin ruminated on the immensity of King's calling and how little time he must have had for love and romance. He had been "waylaid" from the "human course." Romance had once been a priority for Gwin, she revealed in the poem, but not anymore. She too had been waylaid, but she was apprehensive.

> I don't want to see it through
> this mission I wish I could shrink from
> I'm gonna do it,
> At least I am doing it.
> reluctantly
> now surely
> more important than love.
> I may learn to love now
> that's the hope

After the poem's final line she added, "Statement of purpose, February 11, 1990."[1]

One of Gwin's male friends from the Cortland institution walked out of the rehab facility and joined Gwin in Rochester. She tried to get him to engage in life outside the institution, but he soon returned to the New Medico facility. She realized that independence frightens some.

Gwin was dissatisfied with the pace of action by government agencies she had petitioned to look into corruption within the New Medico organization. She and a few other people who had relatives in the rehab facilities started a whistleblower lawsuit in March 1992. Filed in US District Court for the Western District of New York, the complaint was kept under seal. The *qui tam* suit versus New Medico Holding Co., Inc., et al. included Gwin and four other parties.

Almost twenty-seven years later, their lawyer, A. Paul Britton, based in Rochester, recalled Gwin and the 1992 case. Gwin wanted her day in court, he said, and pushed for justice. The purpose of *qui tam* litigation, he explained, is to stand in for the government if you have failed to interest it in standing up for itself when it has been defrauded: "You step in in the shoes of the government trying to seek relief." According to Britton, Gwin was less interested in a financial judgment than in pursuing a way to allow people with disabilities to obtain services at their homes. Billing Medicaid thousands of dollars weekly for forced stays at institutions made no sense to her. Britton met with Gwin at her apartment and remembered her strong personality. "Whenever I see things in the paper about disability and disabled people I think of Lucy Gwin," he reflected. New Medico began selling off its rehab facilities in the fall of 1992 after a government inquiry, and the suit was dropped.[2] Federal authorities later concluded their probe without bringing criminal charges but New Medico had broken up its brain injury business.

At the time, Gwin was getting by, but just. She had virtually no money or assets, her attorney advised a creditor who won a contempt order against her for not making payment on a bank debt. She had $1,600 in an individual retirement account and little else. She was awaiting Social Security disability checks. Eventually she got a $10,000 settlement from the insurer of the person who owned the car that had crashed into her Toyota. The money had to cover lawyers' and an expert's fees as well as advances Gwin had already received from her no-fault insurance policy.[3]

The FBI and the US Department of Justice—two of the many entities Gwin contacted—did eventually take action against New Medico. From late October to early November 1992, the FBI issued subpoenas and raided facilities run by the organization. Agents from the Bureau's Boston office took records from the company's Lynn, Massachusetts, headquarters and some of its thirty-eight facilities in fifteen states. They collected 750 boxes of records from the company's main offices alone. Gwin, it turned out, wasn't the only one sounding off. After a public record request, the FBI released a thick file with the names of complainants redacted. The file shows that the agency received complaints from numerous people. One involved an alleged rape at a New Medico facility in Texas. Another stated that a woman died in a New York facility because of poor care. The raids were so extensive that three federal agencies were assigned: the FBI, the Defense Criminal Investigative Services, and the US Department of Health and Human Services' Office of Inspector General. A federal grand jury looked into false statements and claims to Medicaid, billing for services never provided or not needed, and false claims to private insurers sent through the US mail. One memo identified a former Cortland New Medico employee as a key person to talk to about billing irregularities.[4]

The search was the longest and largest execution of a warrant in the Boston office's history, the special agent in charge said at the time.[5] The FBI file on the case included an anonymous written complaint headed "How to Get as Much Money Out of a Patient—The Big Business of Brain Injury Rehap [sic] According to New Medico." Also in the file was an article from a publication called *PROBE*, a science and media criticism newsletter. Dated December 1, 1991, and headlined "Brain Injury Rehabs Under Fire," the article listed allegations against New Medico and quoted Lucy Gwin, identifying her as one of New Medico's "sharpest critics."[6] It noted that the accusations Gwin had leveled against New Medico were among the claims she would make in an upcoming lawsuit. The article quoted allegations of negligence, neglect, assault, battery, violations of constitutional rights, infliction of emotional harm, and false imprisonment. Gwin, the article stated, had sent a list of witness experiences to congressional panels and state and federal agencies.

PROBE also reconstructed the story of her breakout. The article quoted Frank, identified by his full name, backing up her account. Gwin provided the overall narrative of Frank's interaction with New Medico staff. When he informed them he was taking her home, "he was told I was dangerous," she said, "that he would be responsible for damage I did to anyone . . . He was made to sign a form accepting responsibility for me and any damage I might do for the rest of my life . . . [H]e was told that the police would be called, and I would be committed to a mental hospital, he to a jail. We split quickly."[7]

7

Near the end of 1990, a couple of years before the whistleblower lawsuit, Gwin reached out to Steven J. Schwartz, a lawyer for the Center for Public Representation, a Northampton, Massachusetts, nonprofit legal services provider that works with institutionalized and low-income people with disabilities. She asked him to handle a class action claim against New Medico. The center declined, but Gwin made a lasting impression on Schwartz that affected his legal career and advocacy.[1]

Her numerous calls to him about New Medico's practices raised concerns. As a result, he commenced his own investigation of brain injury rehabilitation centers in the Bay State. He asked questions that led to the Commonwealth of Massachusetts ending its contracts with New Medico. It also resulted in a class action lawsuit and a settlement requiring Massachusetts to provide the option of integrated community homes instead of institutionalization for head injury patients. "She put it on our radar," Schwartz said. "She was a passionate, if not ferocious, advocate for people with brain injuries."

A May 6, 1992, letter from her eventual class action lawyer, A. Paul Britton, to a US Department of Justice attorney, amounting to an apology, spelled out just how ferocious Gwin had become. The letter was sent to the Justice Department during the confidential period when federal prosecutors were working with a grand jury investigating New Medico. Britton's letter to the civil frauds section lawyer involved in the case for the federal government acknowledged that Gwin had leaked a copy of the suit Britton had filed under seal in March 1992. The leak went to a *Boston Herald* journalist who was reporting about New Medico.

"This cannot be excused but it can be explained," Britton wrote. "For more than two years Gwin has spent much of her time and energy in an effort to bring the treatment of head-injury victims by New Medico to the attention of state and federal authorities." Britton revealed that Gwin and her associates intended to continue supplying the government with names and information that could assist in its investigation. "Lucy Gwin believed—correctly, I think—that getting the press to take the matter seriously would be a giant step toward getting state and federal authorities to take it seriously and to take appropriate action," Britton wrote.[2] The letter also disclosed that Britton was dealing with concerns raised by the judge in the class action suit who had demanded to know how the content of the sealed complaint had gotten into the *Herald*, a question that New Medico's lawyers also wanted answered.

The *Herald* scoop was featured on the front page of the paper with a bold headline about New Medico's being "hit" with a suit for fraud. The story reported that the chain had been accused in a "whistleblower suit of bilking the federal government with fraudulent bills." The report further stated that the False Claims Act case had been filed by ex-patients and guardians of patients who alleged that New Medico held people as long as possible if they were covered by insurance and falsely warned relatives that they would assume extensive legal liabilities or that patients would be a danger to themselves if released. New Medico officials denied the accusations.[3]

Gwin kept digging. She developed a network of people critical of New Medico, and used the power of advertising as well as journalistic techniques in gathering evidence. She took out a classified ad that ran in seven editions of the *Boston Globe* in January 1993 seeking current or former employees of "the Lynn headquarters of a rehabilitation chain. Anonymity guaranteed." The ad included her name and telephone number.

As Gwin pursued litigation, and the Department of Justice worked behind the scenes with the federal grand jury looking into New Medico, Congress responded to concerns raised by Gwin and others. Representative Ted Weiss, a New York Democrat known as a defender of civil rights, led an inquiry into New Medico's practices. His Subcommittee on Human Resources and Intergovernmental Relations took testimony on February 19, 1992, in a hearing in Washington, DC, examining the head injury rehab industry. Much of the testimony came from people complaining about New Medico.

On the stationery of *This Brain Has a Mouth*, Gwin submitted a three-page letter to the subcommittee dated February 13, 1992, that was entered into the record. She argued for policies that would let patients live in their homes and receive services there. "Because everything a human being is, and everything a human being does, is initiated, or at least moderated by, his brain, a brain injury can result in any one of one million physical or mental impairments. Survivors of brain injury can possess all of the known disabilities—or none. No two survivors possesses [sic] the same 'nest' of symptoms," she wrote. Her testimony concluded, "Brain injury rehab is a myth—a myth as hollow as it is profitable."[4]

Her complaints about New Medico were supported by testimony from Dr. Kenneth Hoelscher, a former New Medico employee at the Cortland facility. He likened New Medico to a health care enterprise run by Jesse James. Its business model, he said, was built on keeping beds filled even if the patients had no need to be in an institution but had "terrific insurance." New Medico, he testified, was a former nursing home operation whose leaders had realized the company could charge almost ten times more for similar services if it switched to a head injury business. As the notorious robber Willie Sutton used to say, the doctor reminded the panel, he hit banks because "that's where the money is."[5]

Ann Marie Atkins, Weiss's congressional aide, credited Gwin as the original source for the probe of New Medico and said that she provided material and impetus for the investigation. "I was impressed with her gumption," Atkins said. "She put people off a little; they weren't willing to give her too much credibility. If you come across as a little crazy, that is expected."[6]

Later that year, the Committee on Government Operations, chaired by Representative John Conyers Jr., released a report, "Fraud and Abuse in the Head Injury Rehabilitation Industry." Citing New Medico and Weiss's subcommittee work, the report quoted Weiss describing the "rip-offs" by health care companies as "unconscionable."[7]

Bruce Faw, Gwin's assistant at the magazine, recalled going to Washington with Gwin to monitor the hearings. She hoped to influence the elected officials by writing about the problems she experienced, he said.[8]

The lawmakers released a report on their findings that fall and called for a crackdown, citing widespread allegations of rehab companies providing unnecessary care, extending client lengths of stay, billing for therapies not provided, and other abuses. The committee demanded a probe by the inspector general of the Department of Health and Human Services, one of the three federal agencies that had begun raiding New Medico centers across the country two days earlier.[9]

8

Back in Rochester, Gwin was buoyant and emboldened by the federal inquiries. Allies were urging her to drop her Ed the Hothead pseudonym despite the risks of taking on the "medical industrial complex," as disability rights organizer Mark Johnson put it. Johnson reassured her, "It's okay to own it, because what you're saying is true, and it'll encourage others to say it too; more of your peers and allies will say it too."[1] She headlined issue number 12, the May–June 1992 edition of her magazine, as "The Gratitude Issue." It cost $3. In it she revealed that she herself had been the one doing all the dirty work while allowing her alias Ed the Hothead to take the flak for her crusade against the rehab industry.

"Today I take off the Ed the Hothead mask and set it aside," Gwin wrote in her first bylined column. "The battle is not yet over, but Ed has won a good part of it."[2] She blasted New Medico but warned that the chain was not alone in practicing fraud. She'd learned about other bad treatment businesses, some of them nonprofit institutions.

She called Congressman Ted Weiss the hero of the story and ran a large picture of him. She also identified Midge DeMartino as the woman who had helped her launch the magazine two years earlier, though DeMartino took no visible editorial role in the publication. DeMartino's son was a New Medico patient, and her husband worked for the company. "We weren't saints. We only wanted to see justice done," Gwin wrote. "Now two congressional subcommittees and a federal grand jury are bringing the ugly truth to public light."[3]

With the September–October 1992 issue, the magazine dropped the first four words of its name. It became simply *Mouth*. The magazine's subtitle changed as well to "The Voice of Disability Rights."

Weiss died in September, just short of his sixty-fifth birthday. As if she were continuing his hearings, Gwin collected and published more testimony in *Mouth*, but not just from the brain-injured. That fall number 15, "The Speak Out Issue," contained a variety of articles that showed the magazine was broadening its mission: it was now open to anyone with a disability. One article was headlined "I Was Born Crippled and Colored. Now I Am Disabled and Black." The author, Kate Gainer, wrote that she had not attended the March on Washington for civil rights in 1963 but was proud to have been part of the disability demonstrations in the capital in 1990. She declared, "Now is the chance for us to see commonality in our struggles and come together."[4]

In the same issue, Gwin stated in her column that readers praised Ed the Hothead for "being brave." She begged to differ: "I am Ed . . . Ed is neither brave nor vengeful. Determined is a better word. I was and am determined to use the freedoms and rights our nation guaranteed.

"The disability world won't change until our voices are heard," she wrote. She had shouted out the mission of *Mouth*.[5]

PART TWO

Someday there'll be a world without authority, without bureaucracy,
without rules, where there'll be freedom and sharing and love—
and still I won't fit in.
—*Jules Feiffer*

9

Lucy Gwin was born January 5, 1943, in Beech Grove, Indiana.[1] She was raised in a post–World War II Indianapolis that was conservative, religious, and Republican. It was home to people who called themselves Hoosiers and loved living in Indiana. She learned to read in 1945 from newspapers. Her young eyes fixed on stories about the liberation of Jews and others from German death camps. "The Holocaust led me to pledge my energies to the civil rights movement," she wrote in an essay decades later.[2]

Her mother, Verna, was a Louisville, Kentucky, native. Gwin's father, Robert, grew up in Indiana just over the Ohio River. They raised two daughters in Indiana. Bridget was born February 6, 1947, and looked up to her older sister, while Lucy looked out for her. Lucy called Bridget her best friend. In 2006, when she was living in Kansas, Gwin shared a family photo with a friend, using an e-mail address that typified her irreverence: biteme@mouthmag.com.[3]

The photo shows little Lucy and Bridget in tidy outfits and combed hair. Lucy is taller by a head and shoulders. Even taller than her is a boy who accompanies the sisters. Flanking Bridget on the left, Lucy, about six years old, wears a T-shirt with wide stripes, a pleated skirt, and tie shoes. Her lips are pursed in a faint smile. Her frame appears sturdy. She looks away to the left, twirling a string with a toy at the end. A pensive, tiny Bridget in a short-sleeved dress stands in the middle staring at the camera. She looks fragile. On the right in the photo, the boy, a youngster named Mickey, standing a step behind them, holds a string toy like Lucy's, but it falls limp. He has Down syndrome.

The boy in the photo was the son of Verna's best friend, Gwin told her friend in the e-mail. "I feared him when I was smaller than shown here. Mickey the Mongoloid." In a 1998 essay she also revealed that she worried about becoming Mickey. She described her grin in the photo as a "toxic smile" because she was trying to distinguish herself as unlike Mickey, with his perpetually half-closed eyes, his slack jaw, his limited vocabulary. She spent her life "racing to be the smartest, the best-read, the funniest, the most well-spoken, the most sought-after, the memorable, the valuable, the queen . . . Not-Mickey," she wrote nine years after her head injury. As an adult and a brain injury survivor, she regretted her "bigoted" attitude toward the boy. "I am Mickey now."[4]

The girls' upbringing was unusual. Their father would ditch the family for spells. Sometimes he would blow up at them. Once, on a trip down the old two-lane Dixie Highway, he threw everyone out on the dusty red road and drove off in their 1951 Plymouth. Lucy was eight or nine.

Clearly Robert W. Gwin was not boring. Lucy told friends he was a drinker and a gambler, an advertising man with a creative streak. She seemed to be mesmerized by her father and referred to him as "powerful" and "alive." "He made our excitement with his Triumph Parades, his Return Victorious Parades," she recalled in her journal in November 1989.[5] He would pose odd challenges to the children, such as picking up a crawdad for $25. In 2005 Gwin described her father as a "promoter, a bookie, a rapscallion, and an ad man." She recounted how he arranged for a circus elephant to stand on cardboard furniture sold by a client to prove its strength. "He was in the paper almost every day for one thing or another as we were growing up."[6]

In the 1950s, Robert Gwin made frequent use of newspapers. He wrote letters to the editor of the *Indianapolis Star* and Louisville's *Courier-Journal* criticizing President Dwight Eisenhower. As manager of the Indianapolis Industrial Exposition of the Indianapolis Chamber of Commerce, he enticed the local newspaper into featuring his events. Sometimes he would pose for a promotional photo, a sharp-nosed bald man in a suit kneeling beside grass-eating goats or beaming astride a model from a finishing school. One news photo spotlights his daughters. The shot shows Bridget, seven, and Lucy, eleven, amid packets of seeds to be handed out at the expo. They look into each other's eyes with little girl smiles as Bridget "attempts to count the seed packages" and Lucy holds the "jack-in-the-box bunny prize."[7] Later, Robert Gwin worked for Indianapolis Airport Advertising, Inc., and was in charge of a large local children's art show.[8]

One day when Lucy Gwin was five, Verna got her ready for an outing with her father. Verna braided Lucy's yellow hair into pigtails, tied a white pinafore over her best blue Marshall Field dress, and sent her on her way with Robert and his buddies. They traveled to Louisville for opening day of the races at Churchill Downs, where she inhaled the smells of whiskey, tobacco, and horses. The girl cherished that day with Daddy and being among men.[9]

About five years later, the girl had another experience with her father that she wouldn't forget. On a family vacation in Florida, Daddy, likely drunk, asked her if there was something he could teach her to do, she wrote in her 1982 memoir *Going Overboard: The Onliest Woman in the Offshore Oilfields*. She answered that she wanted to drive his car. He turned over the steering and shifting to his daughter. "Sitting on my father's lap on that hot sunny day," she recalled, "was the thrill of thrills for a pigtailed girl age nine or ten." Yet, despite many fond memories of her childhood brought up in the book, she also noted a sign of stress: she was a bed-wetter.[10]

The girls went to Thomas Carr Howe High School, which turned out large graduating classes. Bridget was known for art, music, acting, and poetry. She played violin in a school orchestra. She contributed sketches to the high school newspaper, *The Howe Tower*.[11] In 1963, the *Star* published her photograph and a story about her poetry compositions illustrated with her own drawings.[12] Bridget, with dark hair and a dark sweater, looks up at the camera with a gentle smile. The article noted that three of the Howe senior's poems had appeared recently in a national magazine and that she started writing poetry at age six, when she was published in *Jack & Jill*. The *Star* also noted her art awards and the scholarship she received to study at Herron Art School.[13]

"Miss Lucy Gwin" made the news at sixteen for bringing her Russian wolfhound to a dog show. A photo of her with the big white-maned Domenic shows Lucy with a bow in her curled blond hair. She holds a delicate floral fan in her right hand and pats Domenic with her left hand. Her fingernails are painted, and she wears a crisp light dress. She looks pleased.[14]

In high school, Lucy Gwin did not mix much. She was in the Latin Club her freshman year and was on the Cheer Block, which rooted on the home team, in her second year.[15] The school offered many outlets for many interests, from ROTC and rifle clubs to "feminine" career courses for future homemakers and nurses. At about that time, Gwin ran away from home to join the civil rights movement in Chicago. She took part in a Freedom Ride and a few marches.[16]

Her senior year photo in the 1960 *Hilltopper* yearbook shows a slim blonde looking to the left with a trace of a smile. She wears a light sweater and a necklace. She appears confident, ready to move on. Nearly sixty years later, alumni leaders from her graduating class of more than four hundred students did not recall her.[17] At the time of her graduation, she was pregnant.

10

Just a few weeks after graduating from high school, seventeen-year-old Lucy Gwin became Mrs. Robert Keller. A week after turning eighteen, she gave birth to a daughter, Tracy. A few months after her head injury, she would write in her journal that getting pregnant and married as a teenager were among the top tragedies of her life, along with the death of her dad.[1] Her mother was still alive when she wrote that. Her first husband doesn't like to talk about their marriage. They had a second daughter the following year.[2]

Marc Thorman, a close friend of Bridget Gwin's, recalled Robert Keller as a shoe salesman and "a total mismatch" for his wife. "Lucy was really a brilliant creative person; he was just a regular guy. They just didn't seem right together," Thorman said.[3] Her older daughter, now Tracy Hanes, said Gwin told her that she was drawn to Keller because they were both the children of alcoholics. They had met during high school, Hanes said.[4]

The couple moved to Decatur, Illinois. Gwin started going out to a local taproom, the Winery Bar, where she became friends with a young bartender, Joe Maurer. She would show up in dresses and white gloves. She took an interest in a customer named Phil Douglas. They began a relationship. By 1964 her marriage was over. In her early twenties, a mother of two young girls, she remarried and became Lucy Douglas.[5] Gwin, Maurer said, had walked out on Keller. "She hated that life, hated it!" he recalled. "It's a straight, normal, everyday life like everybody's supposed to like it and live it. Lucy didn't want that." After Gwin split, Keller got the kids.

Even close friends of Gwin's know little about Phil Douglas. He may have sold cars. He may have been in the army. "He had some wicked scars on his body, on his torso," according to Maurer, who socialized with the couple but never got the full story on Douglas's background. "I don't know who knows. And there's a lot of people making up stories in the bars all the time. He was coming on like he was stationed up in Alaska across from Russia and, hint-hint, that they were playing war games up there for real." One evening, said Maurer, Gwin sought refuge with him, frightened that Douglas was going to harm her.

After living in Decatur for a couple of years in the 1960s, Gwin moved back to Indianapolis. Maurer visited her there. He met her sister and mother. He doesn't know what happened to Phil Douglas, but Maurer encouraged Gwin to stay away from Douglas. Maurer distrusted him. Yet in the fall of 1989, as she recovered from brain trauma, Gwin listed "marrying/leaving Phil Douglas" among her life tragedies.[6]

Needing income, Gwin talked her way into an ad agency in Indianapolis and flourished. She made herself so crucial that her employer insisted she take out an ad in *Ad Age* to find her replacement when she landed a job not long after in Chicago. The ad showed her creativity: instead of type, the printed ad featured Gwin's clear cursive handwriting, and it stood out, recalled Chris Pulleyn, a friend and colleague.[7]

After more than a year in Indiana, Gwin was back in Illinois, working at Leo Burnett, a huge ad agency in the Prudential Building on Chicago's Michigan Avenue. She was hired to write ad copy that targeted geriatric consumers of national brands of underarm deodorant and bran flakes.

Pulleyn was nineteen in 1966 and was already a clever ad writer for Leo Burnett. She first encountered Gwin, who was then Lucy Douglas, in an audio recording room. "When I met her, she called herself 'the Widder Douglas,'" said Pulleyn (whose was known by her given name of Martha Christoff in Chicago). Pulleyn assumed that Mr. Douglas had died, but she did not pry. Pulleyn was working on a tune for United Airlines—the well-known "Take Me Along" jingle. Gwin was amazed that the younger woman knew how to operate the recording equipment. She fixed Pulleyn with a piercing stare and demanded to know who had taught her such skills and how much she was being paid. "I told her and she said, 'You're not making enough,'" Pulleyn recalled. Gwin's annual salary was $10,000, $1,500 more than Pulleyn's. They soon were roommates in an apartment building near a shop where a man sold rare birds. Gwin would often frequent the place.[8]

Pulleyn said her memory of the time isn't comprehensive because it was "the sixties," and anyone who really lived through that decade of psychedelic drugs wouldn't remember every detail. Gwin and friends would sometimes drop acid. During this time, Gwin also dabbled in working for an underground newspaper, the *Chicago Seed*, which kept an eye on the Chicago police, the music scene, and the resistance.[9]

Gwin joined a hotshot group of ad writers putting together TV commercials. She became a close friend of Neil Vanover, a heavyweight in the industry. He was a creative director at Burnett and for several other firms over the years and collaborated with Gwin, Pulleyn recalled. Vanover and Gwin had similar senses of humor and high-energy working styles. They pooled their ideas. Once they tried to persuade people to ease their workday stress by taking meditation breaks. They made posters encouraging people to unbuckle their pants, relax at lunchtime, and meditate. According to Pulleyn, the relationship was mentor and mentee.

In 1969 Pulleyn moved to Rochester to study with the Zen teacher Roshi Philip Kapleau, who was based there. Gwin and many others from the Chicago scene soon followed her. But first, Gwin would have to get through 1968, and that wasn't easy.

11

Fred Spears, an Indianapolis native and navy veteran, was dating Bridget Gwin in 1968, a memorable year of war protests and political strife. They moved down to Florida and lived together for a while in Miami.[1] Bridget was the more sensitive sister, not good at parties. She was a poet and a painter. She once made her sister a memorable gift: a black-and-white poster of a chair sitting inside a woman.

In the spring of 1968, Bridget visited their father's deathbed in Florida. He was suffering from a brain tumor and his head had swollen. Robert Gwin died in June. Lucy started calling her sister, urging her to come to Chicago. Lucy pitched a plan of dropping out of the rat race and living in a commune in Oregon. It appealed to Bridget, and less than a month after her father's burial, she moved up to Chicago. Fred Spears stayed behind. That July, he received devastating news: "I got a call in

Miami, and a friend said he'd seen in the Bloomington paper that a girl named Bridget Gwin jumped out a window."

Newspapers reported that Bridget Gwin, twenty-one, had leaped from either the third or second floor of an apartment building in the Old Town section of Chicago. The articles implied that the jumper was a casualty of a drug party. "Girl's Tragic Plunge from Old Town Pad, Round Up Hippie Pals," *Chicago's American* headlined over a pair of photos from the scene on July 23, 1968.[2]

The story quoted police as saying Bridget dove through the screen of an open window in what the article called a "hippie pad." A photo captured the aftermath: Bridget sprawled on the sidewalk with a fireman and a passerby cradling her head, a towel over her skull. The caption said police arrested five youths in "hippie garb" and a sixteen-year-old-girl. "Miss Gwin was taken to Henrotin hospital unconscious." A second photo showed some young men being led handcuffed into a police station. They wore long bangs and long faces. One man's jeans bore stitching in the shape of a heart and other symbols.[3]

A *Chicago Tribune* article on July 24 reported that Bridget never regained consciousness and died two days after her drop from a second-floor flat at 1520 North Wells Street, above the Midas Touch café. The report stated that six people arrested on narcotics charges gave the apartment as their address and that police were looking into whether Bridget was under the influence of drugs when she jumped.[4] It was a tumultuous time. A nearby article in the *Tribune* discussed student uprisings at campuses across the country. Another focused on the death of eighteen-year-old Private Raymond C. Hanik of Chicago, who was killed in Vietnam.

Witnesses at the apartment said that Bridget had taken acid that day, and that Lucy had previously brought LSD to the apartment.[5] Bridget's head had swollen "as big as a watermelon," Lucy wrote later. Although it isn't clear what caused Bridget to jump, Lucy Gwin, in her journal, remarked that suicidal tendencies ran in the family.[6]

Marc Thorman saw it all. He had been staying at the apartment for a month with fellow jazz musicians from Indiana University—the young men arrested after Bridget's leap. His band had been living in the apartment while they tried to make a start in the music business.[7] They were talented, but the band just wasn't succeeding. Their apartment was above a small nightclub, he recalled. Every evening they could hear the same bad vocalist singing the same song, "Going Out of My Head." The place was across Wells Street from a famous jazz club, the Plugged Nickel, and well-known musicians would stop in at the apartment to hang out or jam.

Thorman and Bridget were "soul mates," he said. They had met as teens in Indianapolis. Bridget and Lucy had come to visit him and had been crashing at the flat. He said he was tripping the day Bridget jumped. He remembered being on the floor with Bridget when she rose, ran, and burst through a screened window. Lucy, who wasn't at the apartment at the time, was with Bridget at the hospital when she died, Thorman recalled. After he was released from Cook County Jail, he found out about Bridget's death and met up with Lucy.

"I remember her having a tremendous amount of guilt," Thorman said. "Bridget had gone to Chicago with the purpose of hooking up with Lucy to begin a new phase and Lucy was dragging her feet." Bridget had extraordinary artistic talent, said Thorman, an accomplished pianist and composer who went on to become a college music professor. "It was such a loss." Fred Spears, who became a lifelong friend of Gwin's, traveled from Florida to Chicago to offer help. He learned that it was likely Lucy who had supplied the acid Bridget took. After her sister's death, she fell into a deep despair.[8]

The young men were hauled away to the lockup by the Chicago police on suspicion of possessing drugs after the cops burst into the apartment and found narcotics. Fifty-one years after their release from jail, some of these men still choked up talking about that summer. Not long afterward, the drummer, Eric Long, who was in the house when Bridget jumped, committed suicide himself following a few failed attempts, trumpeter Randy Sandke said.[9]

Others did go on to become professional musicians. Another became a trial lawyer in New York. Some needed therapy and some got it. They had gone to Chicago excited about the possibilities of turning professional. After the incident, they disbanded and went back to their homes, downcast and shaken. They are reluctant to talk about what happened to them during the few days they waited in jail until the charges were dropped, But according to Sandke, who was not jailed, Long was gang-raped there. Lucy Gwin, Sandke said, is part of a difficult chapter in the lives of these men.

"Police determined that the drugs were hers and decided not to prosecute," according to Sandke. In the days before her death, Bridget had seemed withdrawn, while Lucy had been intimidating, somewhat angry. The sisters' plans to join a commune out West, he recalled, had fallen through.

12

After Bridget died, Gwin fled Chicago for a farm in Bloomington, Indiana. Those who remember her during that time say she would flop onto the floor and not get up for long spells. "I was frozen in the memory of that horror, frozen in my blame of myself for the loss of someone worth saving," Gwin would write in 1994.[1] Among Gwin's new friends during that period was Ernie Paul Walker, a photographer with a store in Bloomington called the Blow Up Shop. Walker helped Gwin cope with her pain and became romantically involved with her. He would become another in a line of male friends and lovers who stayed connected to her, but no one else was quite like him.

Walker's best friend was Fred Spears, Bridget's former boyfriend. It was Walker who had called Spears after reading the news about Bridget's "plunge." Spears met Chris Pulleyn at Gwin's farm and became her boyfriend, and eventually her husband. They hung out in pastoral Indiana. Gwin liked to have a weekend getaway during her Chicago years, and now she needed a place where she could deal with her grief and heal.

When he became involved with Gwin, Walker had a young son and was in a relationship with a woman he called his wife, though they never married. He was a bigger-than-life personality who moved from job to job. He worked for the post office and collected garbage. During his postal service work in Bloomington, he took the risk of opening mail from the FBI addressed to students at nearby Indiana University. As a result, he was able to alert student activists about paid campus informants infiltrating antiwar groups.[2] He often relocated and sometimes lived in his car. His son Peter Walker became a dear friend of Gwin's and a childhood pal of her daughter Tracy when she lived with her mother for a time.

When Gwin was distraught in 1968, Ernie Walker shared his philosophy of life and said something that resonated with her: "Resurrection is a sense of direction."[3] He made a lasting impression, and Gwin trusted him to photograph her grieving. A picture he took at the time shows her curled on a bench in fetal position. The photo is from a series Walker shot at the University of Indiana library. The twenty-five-year-old Gwin seems to be gasping for breath, or releasing a sigh.

Another series of photos from this time suggests that Walker's penchant for photography rubbed off on Gwin. She snapped a few selfies. They caught the pensive woman standing before a mirror, a camera in her hand, staring at her reflection.

Thirty-six years later, after Ernie Walker died in 2004, Gwin wrote a letter to his son to console him. Peter Walker, an environmental studies professor, considers it one of the most meaningful letters he has ever received. She recalled her last conversation with Ernie, a few days before he died. She wrote how he framed his philosophy on death as "just an idea."[4]

"When people die, I told him, they are *gone*," wrote Gwin. "We are left without them. Occasionally, I talk to Bridget, my departed sister, in an attempt to say what I did not have a chance to say before she died. She doesn't answer. I am not consoled. Death, then, is her very real absence, not 'just an idea.'" Ernie, she said, then told her something she craved hearing about her sister's suicide: "That's the worst thing, what happened to you, that has happened to anyone I've ever known." He went on, "What I meant by death being an idea is that you [all of us] are a process, not a stasis." She wrote that down.

Ernie told her that not wanting to die was the same as wanting to no longer live, and that if one cannot live, one should die "right," which meant holding onto your perspective to the end.

In her letter to the grieving son, she described how her old friend uttered his thoughts slowly, as if he were stoned—like in the sixties, when they "tromped around the quarries of Bloomington, witness to the quickness of sulphur [sic]-colored butterflies as they danced in sunlit arches over a luxury of Queen Anne's Lace."

Those days in Bloomington with Ernie Walker in 1968 had repaired something in Gwin. Soon she went back to Chicago and joined another ad firm, no doubt helped by Neil Vanover, the creative director whose bond with Gwin also lasted for decades. She concluded that she was a "calamity survivor," she wrote about her rebound.[5] She would become a vice president and a creative supervisor at this second firm, Tatham-Laird & Kudner. "Everybody thought a lot of her," said Rick Rogers, an art director at the firm. "She was a genius."[6]

Vanover and Gwin fed off each other. He was a major figure in the business and was known as the voice of "Ike," of Purina's Lucky Dog dog food commercials and of the bacon-craving canine in the Beggin' Strips ads. Vanover used Gwin to develop campaigns for the more buttoned-up clients, like Procter & Gamble. Vanover's son Charles relished visiting the office and watching Gwin mentally joust with his father. She was so unlike the other women. She wore white overalls to work. Jokes and ideas burst from her.

The Procter & Gamble ad buyers, boring people, would rate the effectiveness of ads by surveying housewives the morning after the debut of a TV spot, Charles said. One of Gwin's P&G ads received outstanding feedback, a Mr. Clean commercial that drew on her insights from years of keeping house. Two of three women contacted remembered the ad, which opened with "Gee, Mom, look at the dirt under the refrigerator!"[7]

"Lucy told that to me twice, so this is her proudest moment in advertising," recalled Charles Vanover. "One of the many reasons she had to leave." She told Charles that the business had become a soul-sapping absurdity. She kept in touch with him for years, and after Charles graduated from college, he visited her for a week in Rochester while trying to find his bearings. He was forlorn, struggling with career direction. Gwin had recently started *Mouth* and was revved up to expose health providers she thought were stealing patients' money, Charles recalled.

She helped him pick himself up. She confided that she had fallen into despair herself in the 1960s and figured a way out. "She had done so many drugs, like I had done so many drugs," he said. "She talked a lot about how she had to reprogram herself. Those talks were very valuable to me."

Charles Vanover became a substitute teacher, then a full-time Chicago public school educator, and eventually a tenured professor of educational leadership in Florida. "She was decent to me, and that basic decency to me was so important."

13

After her hiatus in Indiana and return to the Windy City, Gwin started hanging out with an artsy group of bohemian types. Mike London, a theater major who had dropped out of the University of Illinois at Chicago, was three years younger than Gwin. They became a couple and moved into an apartment house, sharing it with Mike's brother Lee London and his girlfriend Sue Dawson. During this period Gwin also got a chance to reunite with her daughters for a spell. Mike London, Gwin, and her two girls lived on the upper floors. It was the closest thing to stability Lucy Gwin had experienced in years. Still known as Lucy Douglas, Gwin told friends that she had fled a past of ironing white shirts for a used car salesman. "That was not what she wanted in life," said Lee London.[1] Like Ernie Walker, Mike London was funny, smart, and engaging. He adored Gwin. They purchased a one-hundred-plus-acre farm near Dodgeville, Wisconsin. Rick Rogers, Gwin's advertising buddy, bought adjoining acreage. On weekends they camped with other hippies seeking fresh air and the bucolic life on the land. Gwin and London loved birds and bought two crow chicks from David McKelvey, who worked in a Chicago shop. He would later become an author and naturalist appearing on late-night TV shows, including Jay Leno's.[2]

Rogers had a crow named Rudy. Gwin named her birds Ro and Rock, thinking the pets might be able to mimic those names with their calls. The crows had free rein in her apartment, and because they ate carrion, the place smelled like rotting meat. The birds would make the trip to the country, riding in Gwin's red Volvo. When an owl at the farm killed Rock, Gwin accused London of not doing an adequate job protecting the black bird. It was the one time Rogers saw Gwin mad. "She really went off on Mike," he recalled.

London was handy, loved hardware stores, and made many repairs at the farm. He built a window box and erected it outside Verna Gwin's second-floor apartment in Indianapolis so she could watch birds feeding.[3] Despite their closeness, Gwin broke off their five-year relationship after Mike—who died in 2017—asked her to marry him, said Lee London. Sixteen years later, as Gwin was recovering from her accident, she wrote to another boyfriend about Mike, saying he had given her "the best marriage I ever had except we never got married."[4]

Instead, around the time she turned thirty, Gwin decided she needed a change. She quit the advertising business, pledging never to go back to it, and relocated from Chicago to Rochester to become a student of Zen master Roshi Philip Kapleau.[5] Before she left for New York, she gave Rogers the crow named Ro and said her wish had always been to release her birds into the wild. A male crow showed up at the Wisconsin farm, and Ro took a liking to it. The pair flew away, Rogers said, and never returned.

Gwin flitted into an affair with writer Michael Disend. He left Chicago to study Zen in Rochester, and she moved to be with him, Disend said, but he broke off the relationship.[6]

14

Friends, including Chris Pulleyn, had already moved to the city on Lake Ontario to study with Roshi Kapleau. It was Pulleyn's then husband, Fred Spears, who had become a Zen enthusiast and had inspired his wife and friends to go to Rochester to study the spiritual discipline. Gwin and others from her group would follow, including Joe Maurer and Ernie Walker, the Londons, and Sue Dawson. The group became a fellowship of friends and lovers, "a lost tribe," sometimes with Gwin as the chief.[1] Over time, many of them would swap partners and enter and leave relationships among the tribe.

A head-spinning scene once played out at a Rochester maternity ward. Chris Pulleyn had married Fred Spears, Bridget Gwin's former boyfriend. Spears and Lucy Gwin had bonded after Bridget's death and became almost like siblings. Then Pulleyn struck up a relationship with Ernie Walker, Lucy Gwin's onetime boyfriend and Spears's best friend, and became pregnant by him. In Rochester, she fell in love with a Zen enthusiast, John Pulleyn, who became a partner with Joe Maurer, Lucy's pal from the Decatur bar, in a painting and wallpapering business. Chris, who was divorcing Spears, later married John Pulleyn. When she delivered her son, the hospital staff was confused when all the men in her life showed up claiming to be her husband or the baby's father. Spears, Walker, and John Pulleyn were also joined by a fourth man, the birth coach.

Chris Pulleyn, who is still married to John, reflected in 2019 on her years knowing Lucy Gwin, from the late 1960s to the late 1990s. Pulleyn continued to practice Zen Buddhism and became a licensed marriage and family therapist. She came to believe that her former Chicago roommate had "a borderline personality disorder" because Gwin exhibited fight-or-flight tendencies and was often on high alert.[2] According to Tracy Hanes, her mother quit Chicago because she had become bored with the advertising business and the slow times between new account assignments. Gwin eventually grew bored in Rochester, too, Hanes said.[3] But first she showed off some entrepreneurial aptitude.

On the outskirts of downtown Rochester, Gwin opened Hoosier Bill's Homestyle Kitchen. The registration for the restaurant was filed with the Monroe County on January 1, 1973, under the name Lucy Douglas. With the flair of a pop artist and the budget of a Salvation Army officer, she set out to decorate and promote the eatery. It opened later that year with mismatched furnishings painted the same shade of yellow, animal knickknacks on the windowsills, and red gingham countertops. Farm art hung on the walls.

The space was cozy—just big enough for a few tables and a tiny kitchen. It was situated on Monroe Avenue, a major city thoroughfare, in a storefront in a row of old buildings not far from Gwin's apartment. She distributed flyers on colored paper with a sketch that marketed the place as hog heaven: they showed a pig with a halo flying in the clouds and the motto "If you can eat better at home . . . I'll meet you there for dinner."[4]

Although friends said she detested Indiana because of its conservative small-town attitudes, the big picture window of the restaurant displayed a tracing of the outline of the Hoosier State. The restaurant's name was painted diagonally in old-fashioned script through the tracing along with the slogan "Pretty cheap, awful good!" Specials of the day along with prices were posted on construction paper in the other windows. A banner over the door spelled out "HOWDY!" in giant letters. "It seemed to be funded on two cents," said Marjorie Lake, a sous-chef at the restaurant.[5]

Gwin served excellent meals in a homey, informal atmosphere. Customers could enter the tight triangle of a kitchen and order the special or choose selections from a steam table. Many of Gwin's friends and several boyfriends worked at the place. Some of the cooks had trained at the Culinary Institute of America and offered treats such as shrimp purloo or homemade clam chowder.

A November 1973 Rochester *Democrat and Chronicle* article showed a picture of "Hoosier Bill" Thompson, briefly a partner in the enterprise.[6] William M. Thompson, a native of Wabash, Indiana, had been drawn to Rochester around 1973 by the Zen center and started hanging out in Gwin's circle. He was known to greet people with a "howdy." He claimed to be the personality behind the restaurant and Gwin, six years older, was the brains. "Lucy was one smart cookie," said Thompson.[7] He loaned Gwin half his $2,000 in savings to get started. She borrowed other funds from some men from the neighborhood. These lenders drove a big black car, Thompson recalled, and required Gwin to install one of their cigarette machines. Gwin put it in the cellar near the restroom. Later they persuaded her to add a jukebox. Thompson returned to Indiana in 1974 when the Rochester construction job he was working ended. He became a track maintenance worker with the Norfolk Southern Railway. After a couple of years, Gwin sent him $1,000.

His favorite memories of the time involved sharing a flat with three other men near the apartment house where Lee and Mike London lived. His roommates included Spears and Maurer, and a male dog named Rochester, which loosely belonged to Ernie Walker and his son Peter. The sheltie mix was resourceful and brought home much bigger female dogs, such as a Doberman pinscher. Lee London recalled that Lucy Gwin acquired a puppy from a litter sired by Rochester. She named it Who Puppy, or Who for short. Gwin let that dog roam, resulting in run-ins with the local animal control officer. When Gwin was out of town one day, the officer impounded Who and put it down. Gwin was incensed.[8]

Gwin was tough to work for, Marjorie Lake recalled—sometimes sweet and helpful and a moment later a thunderclap of fury. She was a "difficult" person, Lake said, and had self-control problems. But the restaurant was "one of a kind." It seated about thirty and was a regular stop for the Zen students who were in Gwin's Rochester network as well as visiting friends from the Chicago advertising world. Lake credited Gwin with pushing her to take the initiative of calling up a fellow she liked—Joe Lake. She married Joe, they had six kids, and remained together.

"Relentless" was how cook Susan Plunkett recalled Lucy Douglas, as Gwin was known at the time.[9] Plunkett respected and admired her boss's pioneering spirit and was thankful to get her first cooking job at Hoosier Bill's. Plunkett later opened her own Rochester eateries, including the nightclub and restaurant Jazzberry's. "I learned that it was a tough business and you have to learn how to control yourself," Plunkett said. "If you look at Lucy's history, Lucy was an adventurous person who tried a lot of things whether she had any experience or not."

And she had a temper. Gwin once struck waitress Nancy Fairless with a stick on the back of the knees, Fairless recalled. She described her former boss as brilliant, with a "simmering creative streak that would erupt."[10] Fairless, who later married Gwin's friend David Scates, became a girlfriend of Gwin's ex-lover Ernie Walker. Although "Lucy was very good at getting people estranged from her," Fairless stayed friendly with Gwin's older daughter, Tracy, who sometimes worked at the restaurant. Fairless eventually moved to Florida with Ernie Walker and took Rochester the dog with them.

Fairless played a part in a violent incident between Tracy and her mother. Gwin had refused to let the teen get her ears pierced. The girl went around Gwin and got Fairless to sign the authorization. When Gwin saw the piercings, she punched Tracy. "I shouldn't have done that," Hanes said, "but I don't think it also warrants getting hit in the face in a restaurant in front of people we both worked with."[11]

Her mother struck her one other time. Tracy had gone with friends to a roller-skating rink but had not set up a ride home. After Gwin got the call and went to pick her up, she started hitting the girl, Hanes said. She got the feeling her mother didn't want her around. Hanes remembered finding jobs to do at the restaurant, but Gwin would butt in as if to discourage her. "She'd fill the job I was doing," Hanes said. For example, Gwin disliked cooking but took over as an assistant chef after the teen began doing that work. "So I got a job at a grocery store," said Hanes.

Gwin was caught in another complicated relationship at the time. While Tracy was living with her mother and Joel Frank, Gwin's boyfriend, she would hear them fighting through the walls.

15

Next door to Hoosier Bill's, Gwin helped Joel set up another original store, the Tin Rhino. It sold unusual gifts, like glow-in-the-dark rocks, items one could buy for a few dollars, and well-made household goods such as Dutch ovens and Amish silverware. A flyer, sounding like Gwin's voice, promoted the place. It announced its "very grand opening" and came with handwritten ads and sketches of its "misbehaving merchandise": a $9 Polish birdhouse, a $1.10 banana harmonica, a $6.50 piano in a sardine can. The flyer touted the store's "cantankerous parrot" and outdoor sign that belched smoke.[1]

Joel Frank was an artist, a highly ranked bridge player, and a talented bluegrass banjo player, but he was not known as a businessman. He also suffered from bipolar disorder and didn't always take his medications.[2] He was married with a child when he arrived in Rochester in the 1970s. He was drawn by the photography program at the university and by the Zen Center, where he was one of a small group from Ohio's Oberlin College, including Chris Pulleyn. Now deceased, Frank lived with Gwin and Tracy for several months in the mid-1970s.

"Some people thought Joel was a certified nut case, but I'll tell you what, that guy made some sense sometimes," said Bill Thompson. Frank once told him, "It's hard to remember the future."[3] Frank had severe mood swings, and he and Gwin often quarreled. Friends recall Gwin sticking him with a fork during one argument. The fork incident made some question Gwin's mental stability. Mark Seganish, a Zen Center participant and friend of Frank's, said he witnessed the stabbing and Gwin seemed to be the aggressor. Seganish said the couple were arguing during breakfast and Gwin jabbed at Frank's arm, breaking the skin. Someone called the police. When the cops arrived, Gwin switched from a raging screamer into the picture of calm, blaming Frank for the disturbance. "That's what was scary to me, how she could turn it on and off," Seganish said. After the police left, he and Frank walked away down the sidewalk between snow banks. When they heard a car engine roar, they turned around to see Gwin in her red Volvo chasing after them. They had to jump out of the way, said Seganish. He believed that Gwin picked fights with Frank as some sort of psychological manipulation of a weaker man. "Joel was very vulnerable," Seganish said. "He needed a mother and Lucy wasn't that person."[4]

Gwin and Frank broke up. Then in 1978, Hoosier Bill's collapsed just short of bankruptcy after a five-year run. The restaurant, Seganish said, was doing well until a city sidewalk project reduced foot traffic from downtown. The Tin Rhino had closed earlier. According to Seganish, both businesses demonstrated Gwin's special vision. A carpenters' union flooring specialist, Seganish laid the yellow-and-white tile at Hoosier Bill's and helped construct the Tin Rhino. The store might have succeeded, Seganish thought, if Gwin had been managing it. Frank was not up to running a business and spent money on himself instead of paying bills.

Twelve years later, Gwin wrote to Frank, who was living in an alternative residential community called Sonoma Grove Trailer Park in California. She told him about all the writing projects she was pursuing, including her new magazine and a memoir about her experience of sustaining a head injury in an accident with a "drunk driver." Her working title was "Bang on the Head." Gwin sometimes attributed her accident to an intoxicated motorist, although there is no evidence regarding a drunk driver in legal or insurance documents, and the Rochester Police Department has no record of charging anyone with drunken driving in connection with her accident. In her 1990 letter, she seemed to miss Frank. She brought him up to date on some of their old friends from Rochester, including Chris Pulleyn, who she said had opened up an ad agency in Rochester that had blossomed. Gwin said she herself was done with advertising: "Telling lies for a living sucks the big one." She noted that she was a grandmother at age forty-seven but had seen only one of her two grandchildren, and only once. She revealed that few members of the old gang were still practicing Zen. She lamented that she was the only one still toking up—the sole post-hippie hippie. "What happened to hippiness?" she wondered. "What happened to good dope shared among friends with visions of a beautiful tomorrow?"[5]

When she was running Hoosier Bill's, Gwin had written poems to and about Joel Frank. The poetry was a mix of tenderness and torment. In one poem she wrote of hearing "rivers of explanations justifications more than anything self hate" and that "in calm compassion," they could work things out. "You Joel, and I Lucy are on opposite sides. There is too much to say in our favor. Different yes rock and water but good stuff in a steady stream."[6]

In the early 1970s she had tried practicing Zen, and did some deep, daylong meditations—*sesshin*—at a retreat at Princeton University in New Jersey. Led by a Japanese master from California, the *sesshin* involved sitting still and being quiet, with the object of exposing one's demons, said Fred Spears.[7] Instead, Gwin's mind drifted to food, pinball, smoking dope, making curtains, going to the laundromat, she wrote in a journal. She was astounded when the master asked the assemblage, "How do you realize God when driving your car?"[8]

Gwin did not fully embrace Zen like some of her friends. She tried other things, including Rolfing, a form of physical or mental therapy that involves a type of intense, sometimes painful massage. She and Joe Maurer drove to Toronto so Gwin could try a session. Each session was divided into multiple parts, and the program typically required ten meetings. At her first meeting Maurer waited outside while Gwin went into a private room. The Rolfing had just begun when Maurer could not believe his ears. "I'm hearing some horrible, horrible sounds—hysteria and pain and agony," he recalled. "She couldn't even go through the first baby steps of the thing." Gwin walked out and never returned.[9]

Maurer had trauma of his own to deal with—he himself had been in a serious car accident a few years earlier—and he returned to Toronto several times. He completed a dozen sessions, finding Rolfing emotionally and physically rewarding. He credited it with helping him lose weight. But Gwin wanted out after the first fifteen minutes, and her screams alerted him to something about her. "Whatever life handed to her just hurt too much," Maurer said.

16

Taking the advice of her friend "Slammin' Sam" Baxter, Gwin decided to head for the Louisiana coast after shuttering her restaurant in 1978. Baxter had recommended the adventure of finding a cooking job on one of the boats there, and it was a rare case of her following someone's suggestion.

First, she bid good-bye to her daughter Tracy, who had graduated from a Rochester high school. Tracy had opted to live with her father and her sister Christine and a blended family in Illinois. Her dad came and got her. Gwin's daughters would not see much of their mother again. She reasoned that the girls preferred living with their father because he offered the stability of a realist. He was a person whose life did not fall apart every few years. Gwin was at a crossroads, she later wrote. "If I was no longer to be a mother, a restaurant owner, a neighborhood somebody, just who was I to be? What was I for?"[1]

She drove down to Louisiana with her latest boyfriend, a guy she nicknamed Seymour. He was a hard drinker and a painter in Joe Maurer and John Pulleyn's wallpapering and painting business.[2] When she got to Morgan City, Gwin talked her way into a job as a $45-a-day cook on a boat that ferried people and supplies into the Gulf of Mexico, servicing the oil rigs. She planned to adopt the life of a sailor.

For a year Gwin worked the oil rig routes on a variety of boats, first in the kitchen and soon as a deckhand, reporting to a series of captains as a member of crews made up of colorful, uncouth, rugged men. Her experiences became the subject of her 1982 memoir, *Going Overboard*. It was at this time she dropped Douglas as her last name.

Lucy Gwin's US Merchant Mariner identification card shows a slender brown-eyed blonde with an ardent stare. She is listed at five feet five inches tall and 140 pounds, a member of the seaman/wiper/steward's department.[3] In her book she described herself in the vivid, direct way she delivered the overall narrative. "I am not pretty, let alone beautiful," she wrote. "My face is a long flat pan with a prominent chin and an oversized forehead, some cur cross between peasant German and coal-mining Welsh." She estimated herself as ten to fifteen pounds overweight, and thick-boned. She said she had big feet, an unspectacular nose, and a natural mess of hair that was either yellow or brown, depending on sun exposure. "I do like my hands, which are large and useful, with long and literally sensitive fingers. I have a nice voice sometimes, dark and female. But my few good features will never qualify me for prom queen in this age of anorexia."[4]

Yet the men around the oil rigs were attracted to her—those from other ships and sometimes her crewmates. She suffered slights and misogynous jokes. "Never had my nose rubbed so long and hard in the wrongheadedness that constitute male definitions of female," she wrote to her friend Chris Pulleyn back in Rochester.[5] She bedded one of her captains, which turned out to be one of many mistakes she made aboard the three-hundred-ton boats that were her workplace. Some of the men exhibited belligerent, if not sociopathic tendencies. One pushed her overboard in an assault that could have killed her. That experience, and her attempts to outwork crewmates, provided the title of her book. The incident demonstrated her will to live as well. She described fighting to swim back to the boat and scrambling to safety. And she proved she would defend herself: she punched a captain who called her a slut. Not long after, she took a look at herself in a mirror. Typically that would be something she avoided, like being photographed.

She revealed that mirrors scared her. They showed imperfections—a total of thirty-four she counted as an unhappy teen. Her reflection had once spooked her when she was on acid in 1967 and saw her face melting in the glass of a medicine cabinet. On the boat that night, she saw herself staring back and noted she had become slimmer, firmer. "But the mirror woman's black eyes, volcano eyes, warned me off."[6]

The second chapter of the 288-page memoir set the tone for her account of months at sea among people she initially got along with, but with whom things did not end well. She wrote about the horror of Halloween night in 1978. It was about a week before she started working on the boats. That night Seymour came home drunk and angry, complaining that she was leaving to live a mariner's life with a bunch of men.

Gwin and Seymour became lovers around 1976 in Rochester. They had break-ups and rows but found enough in common, particularly pot and sex, to extend their relationship. In January 1976 they were having difficulties when he was jailed and needed bond money. She penned a long letter that was expository and desperate. She referred to her Buddhist vows to liberate and to uproot and to see inside oneself. She wrote of the rounds of pain one passes through before reaching the entrance of "harborings."[7]

She laid out secrets she'd been harboring herself. One time in Chicago she had gone to a South Side doctor, who gave her pills to cause an abortion. "I was the mother of two children I already didn't want—had left," she wrote. She'd had another abortion in 1975, she revealed. The letter seemed to be written in shifts as she got drunk. She marked the time as two a.m. when she unveiled another secret: "I always have awful fights. Nobody wants me. I don't blame them. I'm not surprised you joined the ranks of the formers. I've been unbearable to all men all my life." She told him she'd loved him but questioned what love was other than an "enormous need." She wanted Seymour to know her past so that it would be easier for them to part. "I want to kill myself, quit," she concluded, before a P.S. in which she brought up a night when he'd hit her repeatedly. "Do humans forgive? Does God?"

Almost three years later, as she disclosed in her book, Seymour grabbed her by the hair and dragged her out of bed in the house they shared in Louisiana. He forced her to the kitchen floor and sexually assaulted her using two knives, one at her throat and one inside her. "The rape lasted just a little while," she wrote. "I don't know how long. Just the barest little slice of my life, maybe not even as long as it takes to smoke a cigarette, or pick out a magazine at a newsstand."[8]

17

Gwin delivered an engrossing narrative in her memoir, but she may have boasted and embellished here and there. For instance, her former restaurant's home-style meals became "gourmet." Her position in Chicago became "advertising executive." She described herself as a vice president with an expense account, able to take two-hour lunches and enjoy "profit sharing, stock, the works."[1] She may have gotten facts wrong. Tracy Hanes said her father had not flown in on a private plane to get her in Rochester, as Gwin wrote. He had gathered his Illinois family in a car and driven to New York to attend her graduation. When she told Gwin that she was thinking about rejoining her dad to attend college, Gwin got upset. "She asked me to leave," said Hanes.[2]

Though Gwin worked harder and longer—she called herself "Super Woman"—than most of the deckhands on her crews, she found herself blackballed from the boats, unable to get a post. Her adventure at sea turned into a struggle to find someone to trust. Even a father figure, one of her captains who had mentored her, emerged as a duplicitous character. But the experiences gave her material for her book, which sold in the non-fiction and feminist categories. It also drove her to discover the value of the legal system. She wrote about going into the stacks at a public library to study the Civil Rights Act. She determined that she had grounds to sue for sex discrimination. She contacted numerous Louisiana lawyers. None would take her complaint because they had conflicts of interest or preferred to handle other areas of the law. She wrote letters to the Equal Employment Opportunity Commission, the American Civil Liberties Union, the civil rights department of the Maritime Bureau.[3]

Finally she found someone to take her suit. In the three-paragraph "Acknowledgment" that concluded her book, she thanked lawyers and Bayou Lafourche Legal Services, Inc., for the memoir's being subsidized "unwillingly" by the boat company's settlement with her. She also thanked David Lewandowski, a former Hoosier Bill's chef who came down to live with her when she was writing the manuscript, and Sue Dawson and Verna Gwin for saving the letters from which the first draft of the book was created.[4]

Dawson, Lee London's former girlfriend, remembered receiving the letters and returning them to Gwin for the project. She said that at first Gwin's missives were bursting with excitement at the discoveries she was making on her voyages. Dawson remembered the letter about Gwin's rape, too. She'd go into detail about things she loved doing—such as getting the chance to pilot the boats. Dawson said Gwin had a habit of getting exhilarated over something and sharing her findings, for instance, when she first heard Elvis Costello's songs and urged friends to buy his recordings. With her passion, Gwin could have made millions of dollars if she had stayed in advertising, Dawson said, but that wasn't for her. She dared to take risks, like entering the male-dominated field of offshore drilling. "She was an outsider," Dawson said. "That's an interesting thing right there: Why would someone choose to be an outsider?"[5]

Gwin claimed she typed out her memoir while stoned. "I laughed LOTS while I was writing it," she wrote to a friend, Mary Johnson, in 2000. "They could hear me laughing up and down the bayou." Pecking night and day, she finished a first draft in three weeks, barely stopping to eat, bathe, or spend time with her boyfriend, David Lewandowski. "My sweetie would come home from work at the Avondale Shipyard, lead me into the bathtub and wash me while I read out loud what I'd written that day. Cuz I wrote until the stink literally poured off me. (Do you stink when you really write? Boy, I do. I'm stinking right now for that matter.) Then he'd feed me but had to do it by hand, one bite of beans and rice at a time, cuz I was back at the typewriter."[6]

The publishing world recognized the strength of her words and the value of her story as the "onliest little woman in the offshore oilfields." Viking Press gave her a contract and recommended changing the title from *Unwelcome Aboard. Going Overboard* hit bookstores in 1982 and received some favorable reviews.[7]

Her agent, Rhoda Schlamm, said Gwin stood out among her clients. She liked Gwin and thought her book was a tightly written "page turner."[8] Gwin visited her in Manhattan and was unforgettable. "Very strong personality, witty, acerbic, fine sense of injustice," Schlamm recalled. Viking Press editor Barbara Burn Dolensek said that Gwin was unlike any of the other writers she encountered during her long career. "I just remember thinking she was the most amazing woman I ever met," Dolensek said. "She was tough and, at the same time, nice and able to overcome some horrible things. I remember being terribly impressed and [thinking] that I wish I was like that."[9]

Viking received Gwin's 75,000-word manuscript in February 1980 and in April responded that the story was gripping but needed something else: "We want to know more about you, Lucy . . . Your feistiness, your anger, and your determination are there but we want to see the other side." Dolensek said it seemed Gwin was hiding parts of herself and she had to stop doing that.[10]

In November, Dolensek wrote a three-page single-spaced response to a new draft. "This is a book," she wrote. "You've gotten the perspective while keeping the anger and the joy and I'm very glad about that." She urged Gwin to attempt another draft to make her characters more vivid, insert more background about herself, and reduce the Cajun dialect. The toughest editing demand came on the last page, a directive for more "dramatic tension."[11]

"The book sags in the middle," the editor wrote. There were too many examples of rejection and masculine offenses. She directed Gwin to cut at least fifty pages to make sure readers didn't side with the captains who repressed Gwin "because you were so desperate and persistent." Gwin put the book in shape as directed. The book did all right. Viking issued Gwin a royalty statement for the six months ending October 31, 1982. It showed sales of 2,211 hardcovers, good for $3,503.42 in royalties. She had received a $7,500 advance.[12]

In the *Los Angeles Times*, reviewer Carolyn See praised the book and addressed Gwin directly: "You sneered at them, Lucy, even as you recorded their language and their personalities with a genius-ear . . . It doesn't matter, you got a good book out of it." See opined that the memoirist had a "better career than deckhand waiting for her."[13]

18

The book ushered in Gwin as a woman of letters. She purchased high-quality off-white stationery with her name and address printed in the upper-left corner in boldface: "Lucy Gwin, Writer." Multiple news outlets reviewed the memoir, and the author made appearances on morning network TV shows.[1] Gwin told her friend Mary Johnson in 2000 that the interview she couldn't forget was the one in which Jane Pauley of the *Today Show* asked her why she didn't just quit the boats when she realized she wasn't wanted. The TV celebrity, Gwin said, didn't understand destitution. "I was poor," Gwin wrote in 2000. "Jane hasn't had poverty. How could I explain that to her? . . . I didn't have a toehold on earth. I had to make good at something. Do you know what it takes to uproot and plant yourself again, alone and broke?"[2]

Gwin sat down with reporters to talk about her book. She discussed her background and even posed for photographs. A picture of her in the

Rochester Times-Union in 1982 shows Gwin at her writing desk, a standard typewriter behind her and photos on the wall of naked men who appear to have physical deformities. Gwin stares at the camera with a tilted head, her hair pulled back, and her long hands draped over a crossed leg. In the profile, Gwin, age thirty-nine, told the *Times-Union* that she intended to "make her living by the typewriter."[3] The article said that Gwin sold the option to *Going Overboard* to "Stan Rogo [sic]," producer of the TV series *Fame*, for $100,000. Stan Rogow, who went on to make several television shows, most notably *Lizzie McGuire* and *Flight 29 Down*, remembered Gwin thirty-eight years after signing the deal to use her memoir for a potential television program. He read the book and was struck by the thought that it would make a good show: "The notion of oil rigs and a woman working there and a woman in a man's world—I remember that was the appeal," said Rogow.[4] But the project never got off the ground. No script was ever created and the option lapsed, netting Gwin only $5,000 to $10,000 of the potential $100,000 if the show had been made. Rogow had a vague memory of the actor he had in mind to play Gwin: Susan Sarandon.

The *Times-Union* article detailed Gwin's early marriage to a shoe salesman and her exit from the ad business, saying she had given up the Procter & Gamble account to pursue Zen in Rochester. The reporter contacted Verna Gwin in Miami, who described her daughter as characteristically courageous and having overcome childhood timidity. "She was always a very inquisitive and bright child. I sort of expected things to happen," Verna told the newspaper.[5]

Adweek's write-up noted Gwin's work in the 1960s for the Chicago firm Tatham-Laird & Kudner, where she was one of the "creatives." It reported that Viking hoped to have Gwin's book made into a TV movie. Gwin was busy writing another book, the article said, about human mating habits in the twentieth century. *Adweek* also reported that she was cleaning houses three days a week and freelancing to make ends meet.[6]

Another creative person from the entertainment industry envisioned *Going Overboard* as a motion picture. Trudy Elins called Gwin in 1990 to inquire about rights to the story. Elins, who was a production assistant for comedian Bill Cosby's TV show from 1987 to 1992, was thinking about moving into movie production. Elins had met Gwin a decade earlier in her hometown of Rochester. She had read the memoir multiple times and was enthralled by Gwin's feminist tale of trying to find space in a man's world. The book also offered amusing pointers such as how a deckhand can lasso a post by mimicking a discus thrower, or how a woman can repel unwanted advances by picking her nose. In Rochester, Gwin had befriended Elins, who was twelve years younger and was searching for job opportunities. Gwin told her stories about Illinois and Louisiana and gave her advice, from career tips to insights Elins still laughed about forty years later: To get out of jury duty, declare you suffer from explosive diarrhea. Gwin urged her to go into ad copywriting, handed her a list of ten agency contacts in Chicago, and instructed her on how to write bold pitch letters. That led to twenty interviews. "If she took an interest in you and thought something would be best for you, you darn well better do it," Elins said. A Rochester agency hired Elins, and she wrote ad copy there until moving to New York City in 1984. "She helped launch my career," Elins said of Gwin. When she reconnected with Gwin in 1990, she found out about the car crash and the magazine project. "Drama followed her everywhere," Elins said.[7]

19

One warm day after her return to Rochester from the bayou, Gwin was strolling with a girlfriend in her Park Avenue neighborhood when she saw a man working on a green 1969 Plymouth Satellite. "A 318 V8 automatic," David Arico recalled. He was fixing his ex-girlfriend's car as a favor, and she called him later to say a woman had left a note for him on the Plymouth. It included a telephone number. That was how Arico met Gwin. On a dinner date he realized that Gwin, ten years his senior, wasn't a good match. "It really became very obvious that romance was not an option," he said. Her energy impressed him, though. The two became friends, and he sometimes did work on her apartment. She lent him a copy of her memoir. He recalled how she'd hang out on her second-floor porch with plants and bamboo curtains. "She had manic drive," he said. "I can remember she would get this expression: her mouth would get tight and she would bull ahead and push forward."[1]

In time he met Gwin's new boyfriend, a fellow named Foley, a big guy who was a baseball enthusiast. Gwin would quiz Foley from a thick book of baseball trivia. Since he was a good mechanic, Arico was enlisted to accompany Gwin one time when she was scouting a used car, a Mazda. She needed wheels because she had gotten a job in advertising again. He evaluated the car and gave it a thumbs-up, and she bought it.

Through her professional contacts, she made friends with a couple in a printing business who needed a part-time printer. Gwin recommended Arico, and he got the job, in a building that was next door to the Rochester Center for Independent Living. He met a social worker at the center who was helping people with disabilities. They became inseparable. In 2007 she died of a neurological condition, leaving behind Arico and a therapy dog. Arico credited Gwin's note on his ex-girlfriend's car with leading him, indirectly, to the love of his life.

Gwin continued writing and research for proposed books, often involving people on the margins. She began a work of fiction based on a nineteenth-century story about a person who had two faces. The envisioned novel, with the working title "Mordrake's Other," would be about a man who had a second face at the back of his head—a female "evil twin." In her sketch of the story, Gwin wanted Mordrake to differ from the Elephant Man, whose afflictions were physical or medical. Mordrake suffered from a social affliction, an "open battlefield of the self."[2] Gwin, sometimes so up, sometimes so down, may have related to the dual personalities. Was the concept autobiographical, an indication of self-awareness, or another example of a curious, creative mind?

She drafted other characters for the novel. One was a mother, age sixty-six (Verna was sixty-nine at the time), who was distant, intelligent, and focused on trivial matters—ignorant of the "raw and the genuine." Another character, Mordrake's father, would be "shamed, heroizing, furious, seeking some impossible blessing." The hero, Edward Mordrake, would kill himself at age twenty-three by slashing his own throat. Edward's death would also still the feminine voice from the other side of his head.[3]

In 1980 Gwin set about writing a nonfiction book she intended to call "Women Without Men." A manuscript of early chapters featured two women who had broken away from relationships and were experiencing independence. A third was a lesbian, and that section was excerpted in a feminist newspaper based a few blocks from Gwin's apartment in Rochester. Touting itself as a publication from Susan B. Anthony's hometown, *New Women's Times* published Gwin's article, "Karen: I'm Lucky. I'm a Born Dyke." In it, Gwin noted that she was working on a book about "socially stigmatized women (the 'ugly' or the 'crippled' for instance)."[4] In her book manuscript, Gwin revealed that in 1980 she decided to live without a man. "I have spent twenty-five of my thirty-seven years flinching from it, fighting it off," she wrote, but found man-less life unusually peaceful, spacious, free of personal problems. She called herself "a crusading separatist."[5]

Gwin also wrote an essay called "The Marriage Conspiracy" and gave speeches promoting the theme of independent women. The Women's Studies Department at the University of South Carolina, billing Gwin as the author of *Going Overboard*, promoted her address on campus in March 1985 with a publicity photo. The notice shows Gwin looking away from the camera, her head cocked, holding a cigarette in her right hand.[6] "For many women, being without a man is an almost ultimate horror, right up there with terminal cancer," Gwin stated in her essay. Modern society, she argued, judged women who were without men, and women should be angry when they sensed the question "If you're so terrific, how come you're not married?"[7]

Her treatise, developed during the 1980s, was presented after Gwin had gone through two divorces and married again, in 1983. This third marriage, to John F. Foley, a year younger than Gwin, came with little fanfare.[8] Foley, a United Auto Workers employee and union activist, as well as a heavy drinker, had been on the periphery of the extended "tribe" of Gwin's friends.[9] Foley's father ran the Top of the Plaza, a revolving restaurant that was once a premier jazz venue in Rochester.

They would not live together long, splitting up within a year. Citing "unhappy and irreconcilable differences," Gwin and Foley drafted a separation agreement that spelled out that they would live apart as if unmarried but with the potential for reconciliation.[10] The official separation declaration was not filed with the Monroe County clerk until September 2009.[11]

In June 1983, two months after Gwin's wedding, Verna sounded effusive. "She's so happy," she wrote to a friend. "I'm so thankful that she found somebody she's really happy and in love with." She noted that Lucy had acquired her dress at a Goodwill store. Verna said she regretted not attending the ceremony and wished she could have been in Rochester to see the magnolia trees, daffodils, and forsythia in bloom. Verna's letter featured her hand-drawn envelope art, in the same blue ink as her hand-written note. The drawing was of birds.[12]

20

Despite her disdain for the advertising business, Lucy Gwin began soliciting and getting work again with agencies. Letters to various firms during the mid-1980s—in Buffalo, Rochester, and Syracuse—showed her writing pitches with verve. She began some letters by addressing the president or chairman in a disarming style, affixing a suffix such as "Himself" after the person's name. She would conclude that she would be following up the letter with a call "(and that's a threat)."[1] She wrote that she had been freelancing for agencies at the time, traveling between Rochester and Chicago, and joked about needing to settle in one place so that her dog remembered her.

In the letters, she stated that she had been representing Needham Harper Worldwide in Chicago on a special squad of freelancers that pursued $226 million in new business and succeeded in netting $93 million of it—contracts with Michelob Light, Kraft (a new product), the Clorox Corporation (new detergents), and Sears (apparel)—with another $75 million expected. To one Rochester agency head she wrote: "I'm tired of living in hotels and shuttling home at $400 a crack. And I'm still determined to live out my days in Rochester. But I'm not looking for a regular job any more. (Why should I wake up in the dark to propel myself to a punitive tax bracket, when, as a freelancer, I can sleep in and deduct everything from paperback novels to nail polish? Eat your hearts out, full-timers.)" She revealed that she had been working with a "small, ambitious Rochester agency" on some projects.[2]

That small, ambitious firm was SanFilipo Younger Associates. SYA's clients ranged from local retailers and restaurants to larger corporate customers as well as other ad agencies. Gwin joined as an in-house free-lancer but often misrepresented herself as a partner, to the chagrin of Fred SanFilipo and Bruce Younger, who described her as hard-charging—perhaps too hard-charging.

Her aggressive style helped her firm develop a series of in-your-face promotions for a local pizza shop, setting off what became known as the Pizza Wars. She developed an ad that described a local shop, Mr. Shoes, in phallic terms. The ad suggested that consumers "Bite the Large One," the heavier, bigger slices offered by Mr. Shoes, and eschew the puny pieces sold by a chain restaurant, which was depicted with the Domino's Pizza, Inc., colors. Another ad beckoned customers with a $2-off discount if they ripped the Domino's ads from the yellow pages of the phone book and brought them in with their order to Mr. Shoes. Domino's sent a cease and desist letter.[3]

Gwin helped make SYA more visible. The agency won an award in 1988 from *Art Direction* magazine for an article Gwin wrote on the power of brainstorming. Her essay resulted in a story in the Rochester *Democrat and Chronicle* about Sanfilipo Younger's methods of coming up with ad campaigns.[4] Another piece in the newspaper quoted Gwin and the partners and called the team a "creative hit squad." In the article, Gwin declared that "fear is important."[5]

Despite the seeming success of the relationship, the partners were not getting along well with their associate. They valued Gwin as a seasoned veteran and acknowledged that she possessed expertise galore. But they were tiring of her overabundance of opinions. "She thought so much of her ideas she didn't have any room for seeing other points of view on them," said Younger. "There were some incidents in client relationships that became untenable, embarrassing, unprofessional." In one case a computer consultant wanted the firm to create a newsletter. Gwin refused to write the copy, saying that what the client needed were ads to get his brand recognized. She seemed to view accounts from a big-city perspective, according to Younger. Her sights were sometimes set too high for their clients' budgets.

Gwin nevertheless helped SYA grow and broaden its understanding of the components of an ad campaign. She came up with enterprising schemes. But she would stiffen if someone didn't see eye to eye with her. "You never knew how she was going to react to something if she thought it was ignorant or stupid," Younger said.

Although he and Gwin were never close friends, they socialized at group dinners, where they usually talked about marketing stratagems and work. Years later he could still recall the car that she drove around in—a red Celica.

That car often had a bottle of whiskey under the seat, said Emmett Michie, a poet and friend of Gwin's for fifteen years. She helped him get a job as a novice writer at SanFilipo Younger. He later inherited the job of trying to lure new clients and put together a tape to show off some of Gwin's ad clips. He used some footage from her Chicago years, including a Virginia Slims cigarette spot and a McDonald's restaurant ad. She was a mentor, a former lover, and a valued friend, Michie said.[6]

He met her in January 1984 after responding to a personal ad in *City Newspaper*, a weekly alternative paper in Rochester. The unnamed woman advertising her "fascinating history" turned out to be Gwin. Fourteen years her junior, Michie fell into a romantic relationship with her. Gwin celebrated her forty-first birthday amid their whirlwind three-day first date. He said he broke off the sexual affair because he wanted her as a friend, and she was a good one.

That worked for years. They had long talks, wrote, and drank together. She revealed that her father was an alcoholic and a promotional whiz, and that she had been a shy, promiscuous girl in high school and felt people looked down on her. They were close, but according to Michie, his alcoholism grew out of control. She urged him to get addiction treatment. He lived with Gwin for periods and saw her change after her accident. When he visited her at the New Medico rehab center, she seemed childish and more impulsive, he said, and she asked him to help her break out. He declined.

When she returned to Rochester, she was more herself, but unable to find words sometimes. He thought she was using her immense intelligence to mask gaps in recall. "You would see there were cracks below the surface," Michie said. She persuaded a young brain injury patient named Randy to leave New Medico and join her in Rochester, and the three of them lived at her apartment in the spring of 1990. Michie broke his sobriety and Gwin lost her temper when she saw him drinking beer with Randy. "She punched me, split my lip. And then she immediately reverted back like she was eight years old and was terrified of me. She called the police on me, and I'm the one bleeding," he said. He assumed that in her eyes "I had become her father." Decades later, after years of recovery, and dealing with his manic depression, he concluded that Gwin was a classic case of "ACOA," a traumatized adult child of an alcoholic.

In 1990 Gwin took Michie to a demonstration where people in wheelchairs were zipping around buses. They were protesting a transit company's decision to upgrade its fleet without adding wheelchair-accessible vehicles. It was an affront to those who, like Gwin. had pushed for the Americans with Disabilities Act, he recalled. She talked about how someone else could be the Martin Luther King Jr. of the disability rights movement, but she wanted to be its Malcolm X. "She was on fire about that possibility," Michie said. He eventually went back to school and became a teacher of children with emotional and behavioral disabilities.

21

Just as Gwin's behavior on the job produced perturbed customers and co-workers during the day, her private interactions sometimes left people feeling bruised as well. One time at a party, she put out a lit cigarette on the bosom of Sue Dawson, once a close confidante. Dawson suspected Gwin was retaliating for Dawson's having had a fling with Gwin's lover David Lewandowski when she visited them in Louisiana. Lewandowski had been living with Gwin while she was writing her book about working on the boats, but by the time of Dawon's visit, they looked to be on the verge of breaking up. Dawson had apologized for the affair in a letter, and Gwin had responded. "She wrote me saying, 'Next time I wouldn't invite the vultures to my funeral,'" she said. Dawson, a psychotherapist who specializes in working with children with depression and autism, believed she must have crossed a boundary with Gwin and her friend wouldn't forgive her. Gwin seemed to have tapped into a "demonic side" or a "defense mechanism."[1]

Terri Tronstein Jerry, an ad industry collaborator from Syracuse, New York, would socialize with Gwin and another female friend from the advertising business, Susan Jay, now deceased, whom Gwin helped get a job at SanFilipo Younger. They'd argue and laugh and get drunk together. Sometimes Jerry and Gwin would talk about how suicide would be a good alternative to the blues and aging. Jerry and Gwin acquired terrier-poodle-mix puppies from the same litter. Gwin chose an adorable male and named him Digger. She'd talk to the dog like a human, treat him like an adult, and allow him to come and go as he pleased. Jerry remembered Gwin as "always volatile" and "funny" and recalled that she owned a mink coat. They found common ground in disliking Ronald Reagan.[2]

Figure 1. Lucy-Bridgie-Mickey. Photo taken by Verna Gwin around 1949 in Indianapolis, showing Lucy Gwin (left), sister Bridget Gwin (center), and Mickey, the son of Verna Gwin's best friend (right). (Courtesy of Kathleen Kleinmann.)

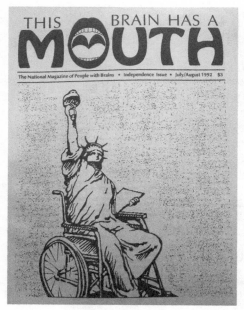

Figure 2. *Mouth* Liberty. Lady Liberty in a wheelchair, in black and white, graced the cover of the July–August 1992 issue of *Mouth* magazine—the "Independence Issue." Lucy Gwin used the image multiple times in the magazine and in posters over the years. (Courtesy of Kathleen Kleinmann.)

Figure 3. Lucy Gwin at her computer at the Rochester, New York *Mouth* headquarters in 1997. (© Alan Farkas)

Figure 4. Lucy Gwin with Justin Dart Jr., May 15, 1998, in Washington, DC. She is wearing the Presidential Medal of Freedom awarded to Dart for his work fighting for civil rights for the United States disability community. (Courtesy of Yoshiko Dart.)

Figure 5. Lucy Gwin (left) covering the National Council on Independent Living conference in Washington, DC, with Luis Roman (center) and Emas Bennett (right) of the Everybody Counts, Inc., center in Merrillville, Indiana, 1998. (Tom Olin.)

Figure 6. Ernie Walker, Lucy Gwin, and Peter Walker (right) at Gwin's farm near Bloomington, Indiana, in 1968. (Fred Spears. Courtesy of Peter Walker.)

Figure 7. Lucy Gwin curled in a chair at Indiana University, Bloomington, 1968, after her sister's suicide. (Ernie Paul Walker.)

Figure 8. Merchant Mariner identification for Lucy Gwin, December 27, 1978. (Courtesy of Kathleen Kleinmann.)

Figure 9. Lucy Gwin and dog, Millie, at a friend's house in Rochester in 1981. (Chris Pulleyn.)

Figure 10. Lucy Gwin at her Topeka, Kansas, home in 2003. (Tom Olin.)

Figure 11. The advertising team of SanFilipo Younger Associates in Rochester in August 1986. From left, Bruce Younger, Lucy Gwin, Fred Sanfilipo, and Krista Keuhn. (© Dennis R. Floss—USA TODAY NETWORK.)

Figure 12. Lucy Gwin with a horse at her farm in Dodgeville, Wisconsin, around 1972. (Lee London.)

PART THREE

Leaders are visionaries with a poorly developed sense of fear, and no concept of the odds against them.

—*Robert Jarvik*

22

Gwin had elder care concerns. Verna was failing in Florida. That triggered thoughts about childhood and her mother's background. Born in November 1910 in Louisville of Welch bloodlines, Verna Bodine Gilcher fell in love with Robert W. Gwin, a fellow almost three years her senior. By 1939 they were sharing a last name. The couple lived in Kentucky and had a daughter in April 1939, but the infant died in May.[1] They set up house in Indianapolis, but they moved often at Robert's insistence. By the time Lucy and Bridget were in elementary school, Verna and Robert's relationship had fractured.

"His restlessness enjoyed new places, new homes. Mama hated it," Lucy Gwin wrote in an intended second memoir. Her father would arrive home about once a year with a bottle of champagne and a note bearing a new address. Verna was expected to transport the family and furniture to that location. "Mom said she hated to see that bottle of champagne coming." But Verna feared abandonment by her intimidating husband.[2] He was exhibiting signs of alcoholism, and before the girls were in junior high school, Verna and Robert were living apart.[3] The Gwin girls graduated from the same high school. Both of them gravitated toward creative careers, perhaps influenced by their parents. Their father worked as an advertising writer and commercial artist in Indianapolis, and Verna performed wonders dressing department store windows or display areas, a second career after having been a teacher. She had worked for years instructing deaf students in reading.[4]

Verna Gwin was hired by big retailers in Indianapolis to construct silk flower arrangements or tearoom decorations. L. S. Ayres & Co., considered the finest department store in downtown, billed her as a "magician," according to an ad in the *Indianapolis Star*.[5] The store employed her to build its elaborate Christmas window aimed at attracting shoppers from a wide region, recalled Fred Spears, Bridget Gwin's boyfriend and a longtime friend of Lucy's.[6]

Bridget Gwin's friend Marc Thorman visited the Gwin household regularly during high school, when Verna was living with Bridget in a small apartment on Indianapolis's east side. Verna was "very kind" and "very inventive and creative," he recalled, sometimes making posters for school projects. She was also independent-minded and became a vegetarian after touring a slaughterhouse.[7] Tracy Hanes remembered her grandmother as always having art supplies—"all these cools things to play with and make." According to Hanes, Verna had to quit teaching because of memory lapses.[8]

In a speech she gave in the early 1990s, Lucy Gwin revealed a family secret: Verna and Robert Gwin never married, although according to Lucy, her mother didn't disclose this information until her seventieth birthday.[9] She repeated it more than a decade later to the oral historian Fred Pelka, who spent a few years interviewing disability rights leaders for his book *What We Have Done: An Oral History of the Disability Rights Movement.*[10] Verna may also have been abused. Both Thorman and David Scates, a friend of Lucy Gwin's, had heard stories about Robert Gwin threatening to strike Verna.[11] Thorman recalled visiting Verna's apartment once when a couple in the flat below were having an argument. When Verna heard the man shouting, she "went down and gave him what for," Thorman said. According to Scates, in Rochester in the 1970s, Lucy Gwin confided to him that when she was five years old, she had to get between her mother and father to protect Verna. Gwin made note of that conversation in a journal she kept at the time: "Drinking with Scates last night . . . [H]e said every time we have a drunk I tell how my dad beat my mom."[12] Robert Gwin may have been an abusive father as well: Lucy told Lee London that as a girl she had been confined to a closet by her father for "wrong behavior" such as defiance.[13]

Verna was always supportive of her daughters' independence. When Bridget, a budding artist, was cohabiting with Spears in Miami, Verna wrote to her: "Remember when you were young you had your tricycle and I let you go down to the first street light and then as you got older I let you go down to the second street light? Now you're going to have to find your own street lights."[14]

Verna loved birds and flowers. In her correspondence, she hand-wrote messages in stylish lettering and in pastel inks, often stamping, drawing, or sticking pictures of animals or birds on the envelopes. Lucy held onto letters from her mother as keepsakes. On one of Gwin's birthdays in the mid-1970s, Verna wrote to her older daughter, "I remember your first birthday as the happiest day of my life—love you even more now."[15]

Lucy Gwin had her own way of defining her mother. Writing down memories in her journal after her car crash, she identified Verna as "the perfect victim," reflecting, "Dad was the raging righteous one. I alternate [between them], and hear mom's voice when I whimper. Dad's voice when I rage is not so clearly heard." She reminisced about her mom's hobby of making puppets and her practice of hanging dolls on the wall. From the string of memories she jotted down "Daddy's hobby of leaving us" and recalled, "If anybody crossed Daddy, Mom believed, he'd walk out and never come back. She was probably right. The time we forgot his birthday, he didn't speak to us all the way to Florida. I was ten, Bridget was 6."[16]

When her mother died in 1989, a wave of guilt washed over Gwin. She felt miserable about having placed Verna in a nursing home. And she thought about her mother's wish to be killed and how Gwin considered drowning her. Instead, Gwin had allowed a do-not-resuscitate order for Verna, something she would come to regret a few years later.[17] Gwin's eulogy for her mother's funeral in Indianapolis was akin to a love letter. In it she touched on Verna's passion for birds and other animals—how she made a mousetrap that wouldn't harm the mouse. She recalled her sensitivity, caring nature, love of family, eccentric charm. The essay was an example of much of Gwin's writing pre- and post-accident: "What I hope to accomplish by this speaking is to restore dignity and honor to her memory, to finally defeat the illness that stole her dignity, her honor, her very fine mind."[18]

She wrote in the eulogy that Verna moved through life with a gentle humor, recalling the time when they moved to a second-floor apartment after Robert left the family. Lucy was nine, Bridget was five. Verna had set up a workroom on a porch, and one day someone's runaway monkey tapped on the window. Verna gave it a banana and went back to her day: "Pure Verna." She also recalled how her mother worked as a teacher for thirty years, first with deaf students and then, in her final year of teaching, with terminally ill youngsters. Verna cried every night that year and quit the profession.

Such were the memories that were running through Lucy Gwin's brain in the days before the two-car crash that changed her life. The collision came in the wake of other disquieting thoughts—thoughts of suicide. In the two chapters she produced of "Bang on the Head," the working title of her unfinished 1990 manuscript about her accident, treatment, and lengthy recovery, and in other writings, Gwin suggested that with her mother's death, she felt free to do what she had been putting off since Bridget killed herself: "I would like to die now, I thought that night in 1968, but I must live, live in pain I will if I must, until Mama dies. Then I will be free to take my own life." She had vowed not to make her mother bear the burden of two suicides. Now, having buried her mother, she went to bed thinking about her "overdue bill."[19]

23

Gwin's thoughts while she was recovering from the traumatic accident spurred numerous journal entries. "I didn't think people got well from brain damage," she wrote on November 6, 1989. "Thought Bridget would be 'better off dead,' same with Mom, same with Dad. Felt guilty for not offing Mom. It's like the events of my life have posed a major riddle. And I'm living the answer."[1] Several entries reveal emotional turbulence. But even before the crash, Gwin detailed her dark side. When she was still a year away from brain injury and Verna's death, Gwin penned a suicide note. It listed all of her assets and who should get each one. It was a modest list. It included the Toyota that she later totaled in the accident. She put its value at "?"[2]

In neat handwriting, Gwin set down her list—not in the notebooks or typed pages where she otherwise chronicled her life, but on graph paper consisting of blue boxes on a white background. She itemized her possessions: $5,500 IRA, $4,100 checking account, $1,300 savings, a copier, a Mazda estimated at $400. Then she jotted down liabilities, topped by $12,280 owed on the Toyota. Gwin named ten "out of towners to notify," including her longtime friends Ernie Walker, Neil Vanover, Sam Baxter, and David Lewandowski as well as her drinking buddies Susan Jay and Terri Tronstein (who later became Terri T. Jerry). "Tell them all that they saved me, that I'd have done this long ago if it weren't for them. It's been a temptation and a comfort for me—suicide—since I was 5 years old. 40 years later, I welcome this old friend. I'm empty; there's nothing more I want to say or do or be. The same ghosts who've haunted me all these years haunt me still—loneliness, fear, despair. They're over for me now, done."

In her distinctive cursive, she detailed her wishes: "I'd appreciate the papers & files being trashed without being perused. Get rid of it." She wanted her daughter Christine to get the Toyota and any household goods she desired. In all, Gwin named sixteen people, specifying that "Joe and Liz [Maurer]" should get her plants and the answering machine and "Fred" (probably her ad business associate SanFilipo) should take the rower. Bruce and Fred (her ad agency associates) could keep the copier. Her friend at the ad firm and former lover Emmett Michie could have the Mazda. Dave Arico, she wrote, could probably use the washer and dryer and noted that he had some things stored in the attic.

She added a directive for her third husband: "Foley gets to pay for the funeral. Tell him to get a very cheap one. I prefer cremation & obscurity. It's cheaper than divorce." The note dates from around May 1988, as Gwin stated that the June rent had been paid so her survivors could take their time picking through her things.

How Gwin got past this low point, this moment of self-pity or this depression, is unclear. But she did see a therapist around this time. She told him she needed a purpose. She hadn't realized this need to fill her empty life until it "escaped from my mouth," she later wrote.[3]

24

Within a few weeks after she broke out of the center run by New Medico in the summer of 1989, Gwin connected with Ken Collins. A former pitcher in the Milwaukee Brewers minor league system, he had suffered a brain injury on the last day of 1976, when he drove a snowmobile into a car, ending his athletic career. He became a member of the survivors' council of the National Head Injury Foundation and had grown disenchanted with the stereotyping of brain-injured people by caregivers, health care providers, and the foundation itself.

He found an ally in Gwin. They worked to change the attitude and the name of the organization: it morphed into the Brain Injury Association of America. The pair, however, thought it was too much under the control of providers who viewed brain-injured people as needy. Gwin and Collins fought over ways to achieve their common goal of reforming the foundation. She wanted them both to resign from the council in protest over the organization's ties to the rehab industry and hung up the phone on Collins several times because he didn't agree. He thought he could change things from within. She had no patience with such an approach.

"She had the balls to speak out about the corruption and she could speak out and say that people with brain injuries—that we're capable, that we're competent, that we can do things," recalled Collins.[1] Among the things he and Gwin disliked was the foundation's logo. It showed caregivers looking down at a patient in bed. The patient had a slash over his head, suggesting impairment. It cast the patient as diminished, they thought. They got it changed to a series of three stylized heads, placing patients, professionals, and caregivers shoulder to shoulder.

Gwin started writing about her brain injury and her New Medico experience with a book in mind, and perhaps a movie. She reached out to some of the people she had worked with a decade earlier when Viking signed on to publish *Going Overboard*. She sent drafts of early chapters of her proposed memoir "Bang on the Head" to her agent Rhoda Schlamm, who agreed to pitch the proposed book.

In a July 1990 letter to a Viking editor, she enclosed Gwin's two chapters. The veteran literary agent described the manuscript as her client's "second survivor story." The planned book would tell Gwin's account of her escape from the "IBM of the rehabilitation institutes" and provide an inside look at the shabby treatment of brain-injured patients. "As an evocative writer and head-trauma victim, Lucy is able to articulate the disorientation of that experience and the tough road back like few can, or ever try to do," Schlamm wrote.[2] Gwin promised the entire manuscript could be completed by year's end.

The prose in her drafts was as sharp as, if not sharper than, in her debut book, and the story was at least as compelling. Her Viking contacts had moved on, however, and the people who had replaced them were unenthusiastic. Gwin thought that publishers, as well as some journalists, did not want to touch a topic as hot as alleged insurance fraud and were unwilling to take on a powerful rehab chain. The project never took hold. Gwin instead turned to her magazine to get the story out.

25

Head injury survivor Billy Golfus was a writer, director, and producer whose award-winning autobiographical film *When Billy Broke His Head . . . and Other Tales of Wonder* made him a renowned activist. Gwin wanted Golfus to write for her magazine and recruited him with unusual terms. "She called me up and offered me a blowjob," Golfus said.[1] He became one of the regulator contributors, furnishing firsthand tales of dealing with disability. His two-part article "Brain Damaged Blues" ran over two early issues of *This Brain Has a Mouth*.

An entry in Gwin's 1989 journal supports Golfus's recollection. She mentioned her admiration for Golfus's talent, and revealed her skill in analyzing writing. It took her some time to get used to his style and rhythm, she admitted. But once she could "hear it," she marveled at "his distance from the first person, you don't notice the 'I's.'" And, she noted, she had offered him "free room, board & blow jobs."[2] Although they never had a sexual relationship, Golfus said they became close over long-distance telephone calls.

He did meet her a few times when she came to Minneapolis. A mutual acquaintance, Colleen Wieck, would bring Gwin to see him sometimes, he said. Wieck, executive director of the Minnesota Governor's Council on Developmental Disabilities, was a supporter of the magazine and provided public funds for Gwin to keep publishing. Wieck also helped get some anonymous articles printed in Gwin's magazine. "She was a natural organizer," Wieck said of Gwin.[3]

Gwin assembled many writers, photographers, cartoonists, and graphic artists for the magazine. Some were members of Disability Nation; some were parents of youngsters with disabilities. Many were being published for the first time and needed guidance. Gwin nurtured and encouraged but also pushed them. Some contributors were compensated, but most were not, and Gwin struggled to pay the bills as she came up with new projects to raise awareness of the inequities experienced by people with disabilities.

Her magazine, which challenged power and insisted on implementation of the 1990 Americans with Disabilities Act (ADA), played a vital role, Wieck said, so she promoted it and helped find money to back it. So did many other readers, some of whom even worked for government agencies targeted by Gwin. Executive directors, commissioners, nonprofit leaders, and individuals dipped into reserves, public coffers, or private accounts. Gwin would thank them in her column at the back of the magazine and list the names of those who didn't mind the exposure. And she made sure readers who couldn't afford a subscription continued to get *Mouth* at a discount, if not for free. She also provided large-print versions and audiocassette options for the vision- and hearing-impaired.

Most of the writing contributors were freelancers. A few live-in staffers resided at Gwin's succession of homes, all known as the "Mouth House," either for periods of months or during a working vacation, particularly when she lived in Rochester. Gwin's rooms held piles of books and office supplies. She decorated with numerous objects in red—oven pads, kitchen utensils, napkins—in a shade reminiscent of early color TV shows. One lodger, Kevin Siek, moved from Kansas to Rochester and bunked in Gwin's third-floor attic. Siek remembered meeting Gwin at national actions, where people with disabilities would picket and demonstrate at government offices to demand equal rights or assert ADA provisions, risking arrest.

Siek wrote a piece for the magazine, and Gwin offered him a chance to become a regular contributor. At the time, the staff included Tom Olin, a photographer who had been documenting the disability rights movement for years. He lived on the first floor of the Mouth House, occupying the flat Gwin's friend and resident handyman "Slammin' Sam" Baxter had previously rented.

Baxter, restless in Rochester, moved to Norfolk, Virginia. On Gwin's recommendation, he contacted Hope House for a job there. The foundation, which runs group homes for people with developmental and intellectual disabilities, hired Baxter and his girlfriend as house parents.

Knowing what clients needed, he set up a remodeling company specializing in modifying dwellings by widening doorways, lowering cabinets, adding railings, and building ramps that were more sophisticated than the rudimentary one he had constructed with crates at the Rochester Mouth House. Hope House appointed him its maintenance coordinator. "She helped me find a purpose in my life," said Baxter, who first met Gwin when he responded to a handwritten sign in the window of Hoosier Bill's advertising for a dishwasher.[4]

After Tom Olin moved into Baxter's apartment in Rochester, the photographer continued making it part of the *Mouth* headquarters. Olin was a calming influence on the operation, as well as a barbecue master when not using his camera. Olin also helped Siek deal with homesickness.

Gwin directed Siek, a novice at advocacy journalism, and set high standards. On one assignment Gwin told him to call Justin Dart Jr. A major figure in the movement, Dart, onetime Reagan administration head of the Rehabilitation Services Administration, had been leading rallies and traveling around the country calling for disability rights. Advocates considered Dart perhaps the single most important leader behind the Americans with Disabilities Act and described him as a Martin Luther King Jr. figure in a wheelchair.

Siek knew of Dart but was terrified at the idea of interviewing him. "I'm just some little nobody. Why would he talk to me?" he recalled wondering. Gwin responded, "Tell him you're working for me." Siek, nervous, made the call. "Justin was just so gracious on the phone. We had a really good interview. And he was like, 'Be sure and say hi to Lucy.'"[5]

Siek also recalled Gwin's pet ferrets that roamed the attic, leaving their droppings where he would step in them. He stayed only a few months in Rochester, as he needed to return to his wife, who had muscular dystrophy, in Kansas. Gwin would stay in touch for years and eventually would live near Siek again when she moved to Topeka. He went back to school to get training on desktop publishing and Web design. That knowledge, and his *Mouth* experience, earned him a job with the Topeka Independent Living Resource Center, propelling a career serving people with disabilities. He helped form a chapter of ADAPT (a nationwide network of disability rights advocates) in Kansas with his wife and the leader of the independent living center. Gwin came to admire that center and that director—so much so that in late 1998 she moved to Topeka and would publish *Mouth* there for the next nine years.

26

Before that westward migration, Gwin seemed wedded to Rochester, which enjoyed a robust economy with mighty technology and manufacturing businesses such as Bausch & Lomb and the Eastman Kodak Company. It was also a suitable base for a disability rights publication, having been the home of legendary revolutionaries and radicals. Women's rights leader Susan B. Anthony had been arrested in the city for trying to vote in 1872. And 143 years before *Mouth*, Frederick Douglass published his abolitionist journal *The North Star* there. His newspaper bore the motto "Right Is of No Sex—Truth Is of No Color."

In 1993 Gwin read a research paper that spoke to her of truth. Written by advocate Nancy R. Weiss, it detailed what she considered torture of children with autism and developmental disabilities at a facility in Providence, Rhode Island. The paper described youngsters in restraints, subjected to electric shock as punishment, spankings, cold water sprays, and other aversive methods.

Gwin introduced herself to Weiss in an urgent telephone call not long after, Weiss recalled. "She said: 'I'm sitting here with tears running down my face. You and I are going to close this place down.'"[1] They made a plan. Gwin placed an ad in the *Providence Journal*, soliciting former employees of a "behavior modification facility" to call a journalist named Lucy Gwin at her home number, which she listed. Gwin got almost 250 calls, and the two women conducted some joint interviews by phone, with Gwin cursing at and hanging up on anyone who defended the facility's methods.

"These calls were so painful, so human and true, so difficult to hear, that it got to where I had an attack of diarrhea every time my telephone rang," Gwin recounted in a speech in Minnesota about the project.[2] In a six-page spread, Gwin published a version of Weiss's paper in the March–April 1993 issue of *Mouth*. The cover showed a Bruce Faw drawing of a person in a shock helmet, tied down to a wheelchair at the waist, arms, and ankles. The title of the issue was a word Gwin made up: "Handicaptivity."

She and Weiss furnished CBS with their interview findings, which led to the network's *Eye to Eye with Connie Chung* picking up the story. On March 3, 1994, Chung dedicated most of the show to the facility and its controversial treatments.

"It happened because of Lucy," said Weiss, who dealt with CBS producers to help develop the story. Weiss later became executive director of TASH (the organization once known as The Association for the Severely Handicapped). and was subsequently appointed the director of disability initiatives at the University of Delaware. Despite their efforts, Gwin and Weiss were not able to shut down the Behavior Research Institute.

Tom Olin considered the work during the Rochester period some of *Mouth*'s finest. Gwin could be combustible. But he and she worked well together. They brainstormed nearly all their waking day and arrived at courses of action and themes for each issue. Olin, with his easygoing manner, performed the art of getting along. He lived under the same roof with Gwin about as long as her three husbands—combined. Despite the close quarters, Olin learned about only bits of her past. They were friends and colleagues, not lovers.

"Most of the time we both believed we were in a war and the enemy was the government or people who were putting people with disabilities in nursing homes," Olin said. "Most of our conversation was about disability. All of our friends were in the disability movement."[3] Dyslexic, he specialized in telling stories with his photos. He lived with a variety of disability movement leaders before and after joining *Mouth*. He knew the issues, the people in the field, the way to approach donors for funding. He also knew he was working beside an intense, driven person who could help make a difference. They had a common goal: to change the world.

Olin loved upstate New York and the Sears kit home that was the Mouth House. He would sometimes sleep on its big porch and watch Gwin commune outdoors with the crows. He and Gwin took trips together to evaluate distant centers for independent living. The trips provided data they could use in a running feature in the magazine, "the bestest and worstest CILs." They would show up at a center and eye the premises and demand to see the IRS records that nonprofit organizations are required to make public so they could review its finances. They traveled in an old Chrysler Town & Country station wagon with seats like couches. Sometimes they would stop to admire and listen to a group of crows. Gwin would imagine what the birds were saying to one another.

On warm summers days, they enjoyed local outings. They would drive to a nearby spring-fed pond to cool their bodies. They would bob along in inner tubes, Olin fishing, Gwin writing, smoking, reading. She was always working, even while floating over a reflecting pool under a sunny sky.

Joe Ehman was another *Mouth* staffer. Gwin hired Ehman to work at the magazine after he rolled the six blocks to her house in his wheelchair. He initially planned to blast her for *Mouth*'s condemnation of the Muscular Dystrophy Association's style of advocacy, including comedian Jerry Lewis's famous telethons. She detested Lewis and denounced his portrayal of people with disabilities as persons to be pitied. The Muscular Dystrophy Association's Rochester chapter had just awarded Ehman Person of the Year honors, and he intended to defend the organization. He confronted Gwin. She said she didn't have time to talk; she was on her way to a conference. She gathered a bunch of documents and dropped them in his lap and told him to read what had been the basis of her reports.

He called her less than a week later and started working for her that day, taking over the "bestest and worstest CILs" column. When he began asking pointed questions of caregivers, the Muscular Dystrophy Association rescinded his award. Although he wasn't paid by Gwin other than a coffee or lunch now and then, Ehman said Gwin taught him more about writing than any of his college and high school teachers, and she opened his eyes to advocacy journalism and the possibility of ending his reliance on disability payments.[4]

He covered a protest in Washington, DC, for *Mouth* and gradually became a spokesman at demonstrations, taking on the "role of wearing blazers and dealing with reporters. Reporters are more comfortable talking to people who look like them." At one demonstration he met the director of an independent living center in Denver, who offered him a job. It was the beginning of a career in disability rights organizations. He eventually opened his own business running training programs in Mexico, but he never forgot Gwin and her energy. "She was always five steps ahead of everybody," Ehman said.

He recalled that when he was dealing with a severe speech impediment as a child, his mother chained herself to his schoolhouse and
demanded he be educated as a regular student. Gwin was like his mother,
he thought—insistent and with a flair for the dramatic. "She was brilliant
in terms of her vision on disability and what it took, what it was going to
take for the community to get what we needed—passionate and angry.
She would have periods of anger—it was like being ten feet away from
a tornado."

Once, Gwin organized a local protest in Rochester. She marshalled
the staff and rounded up some activists to camp out at Genesee Hospital,
where Lillian Conlon, *Mouth*'s bookkeeper, was being held against her will
in its psych ward. Gwin called the local media and stirred up attention
for the sit-in. She insisted on a meeting with the hospital president and
demanded the release of Conlon. After hours of pushing and pressuring,
including calls and faxes to the hospital from dozens of Gwin's allies, the
administration agreed to meet with Gwin's camp. In the middle of that
meeting, the telephone rang. It was Justin Dart Jr. on the line. An aide to
the hospital administrator took the call and was soon in tears because of
Dart's directness. "He speaks like a biblical prophet," Gwin wrote in the
May–June 1996 issue of *Mouth*. "He doesn't scold. He energizes people to
do right. He probably called us patriots."[5]

Gwin and her allies were back the next day. Police threatened to
arrest Gwin and Olin, and they finally did, the only time Olin, who usually
assumes the role of photojournalist, was arrested at a protest. "Lucy took
a lot of this stuff really, really personal, [as if] it was her responsibility to
resolve all of these problems," said Ehman. George Ebert, the head of the
Mental Patients Liberation Alliance who had joined the protest to support Gwin, was arrested too. Although Gwin did not identify as having a
psychiatric disability, he later said, she was so passionate about survivors'
rights that he invited her to be on the board of directors of his mental
health advocacy organization. She turned down the offer, explaining that
Mouth was taking all her time.[6]

Conlon remained in the ward several more days, and that was
fine with her family, according to the oldest of her six children, Patricia
Kolomic. Gwin and the others in the sit-in probably did not know, but
Conlon had been involuntarily hospitalized after pulling a gun on her

elderly parents. At the time, Conlon, who died in 2008, was divorcing her abusive husband, dealing with breast cancer, and caring for her mother and father, whom she didn't get along with, Kolomic said. The family found out about the protest by seeing the coverage on television. An article also appeared in the local paper. The reports showed about fifteen people camped outside the hospital. "It was nice but misguided," Kolomic said.[7]

Yet Gwin had demonstrated her ability to channel her sense of outrage and urgency into rallying the troops to a cause.

The magazine's contents reflected her attitude. Many issues included profiles that introduced leaders in the movement in Q-and-A interviews or in features. These snapshots recognized top officers of the group ADAPT. Americans Disabled for Accessible Public Transit was formed in the 1980s to push for equal access to buses and to demand that lifts be installed. After accomplishing that goal within a decade, ADAPT changed its full name to Americans Disabled for Attendant Programs Today, targeting local, statewide, and national legislation that improves housing, employment, training, and living conditions for people with disabilities. National and statewide ADAPT demonstrations—called "actions"—drew regular coverage in *Mouth*, and ADAPT leaders were much quoted and photographed.

Other articles brought attention to myriad social justice activists and academics and gave them a platform for their ideas and messages. Many of these were written by an emerging journalist who was developing her own voice for activism. An English major in college, Josie Byzek was in her late twenties when she submitted a piece for *Mouth* and Gwin asked her to join the staff. That led to a flow of articles from 1994 to 2001 and multiple trips to Rochester from Byzek's home in Pennsylvania. She spent vacations at the Mouth House writing and learning Gwin's brand of reporting. Gwin mentored her, and she took mentoring seriously, sending Byzek books and tapes, writing thank you notes, sharing her Rolodex, and taking time to instruct her on ways to strengthen stories.

Byzek, tentative at first, grew confident and noticed how Gwin used her advertising background for "advo-journalism."[8] Spurred by Gwin, the young writer interviewed luminaries in the movement, such as Dart and his wife, Yoshiko, and career organizers like Shel Trapp. "I've never won anything by being nice," Trapp told Byzek. "Being nice just doesn't cut it."[9]

PART THREE

Gwin tended to be kind and generous, Byzek recalled, but she could flare into indignation. In July 1995, Gwin and Olin threw a back-yard barbecue to celebrate the fifth anniversary of the Americans with Disabilities Act. Byzek brought her five-year-old daughter. While exploring Gwin's second-floor flat, the girl and a seven-year-old boy put Gwin's two ferrets in cages they found there. Gwin was displeased. She reprimanded the children: "I wouldn't put your grandmother in a nursing home. Why would you put them in a cage?" Another time, Byzek and her family stopped by to say hello and left their pet dog in the car with the windows cracked. Peering down from her apartment, Gwin threatened to break the car windows.

"There are certain people who are elemental, and she was one of them," Byzek recalled. "And if she was an element, it would be fire. There was this creative hum around her. She was unabashedly brilliant, and very pure in her thought. She would see how things would be and not take any excuse for why they were not to be."

It took some courage, and Gwin's pushing, for Byzek to write a commentary for *Mouth* that expressed something she had been thinking about for a while after attending ADAPT actions and growing skeptical about the group's protest practices. Gwin ran Byzek's piece "What's Wrong with This Picture?" over four pages with Olin's photographs. Characterizing ADAPT as straying from the philosophies of Gandhi and Martin Luther King Jr., Byzek criticized ADAPT's methods of surrounding government buildings with protesters in wheelchairs so that the public could not get in and government workers could not get out. Cops who arrested and carried away protesters and their two-hundred-pound wheelchairs risked injuries. Such tactics represented violence and were the opposite of civil disobedience, she argued. She charged ADAPT's leaders with being undemocratic and closed to new ideas from outside their inner circle. She worried that they were leading an all-important movement down a dead end.

In the middle of the commentary, she suggested that ADAPT should not use anger as the cornerstone of its drive for change. She brought up Gwin. "What's below her abundant and well-articulated anger? I pried it out of her one night. Despair, she told me. A deep well of despair that I'm afraid will drown her. She despairs that we'll never free people from

75

nursing homes, personal care homes, group homes, mental institutions, 'sheltering' parents, and a medical system that would rather we die than spend its precious time and energy patching us up, helping us live."[10]

Byzek's opinion piece was one of several in *Mouth* over the years that took aim at a disability rights organization that the magazine normally held in high regard, but with which Gwin or her writers still found fault. It drew an "avalanche" of reader responses, as Gwin put it. Many offered praise, siding with the ideal of love over anger. Others explained that ADAPT's militancy had grown out of its being a faction of a larger group of people who were unwilling to join the movement openly. Several other letters arrived from ADAPT leaders who were less supportive. Marsha Rose Katz of Montana defended the organization, with all its "human imperfections," declaring that it was with love as well as anger that she fought to free people imprisoned in nursing homes and institutions: "Love and anger are not mutually exclusive, and anger is not a dirty word, or a bad thing to feel."[11] According to Kathleen Kleinmann, treasurer of *Mouth's* holding company, the Byzek article caused some subscription cancelations.[12]

Byzek wound down her involvement in *Mouth* by the end of 2002. She had learned a lot and appreciated that the magazine was magnifying and documenting the history of the movement. But it was time for a change. She became a writer for *New Mobility*, a magazine for which Gwin had done some freelancing, including an article on the horrors of nursing homes. Byzek climbed the ranks to executive editor of the magazine, which is owned by the United Spinal Association. "Lucy taught me everything she knew," Byzek said. Before the Internet, and at a time when many persons with disabilities were isolated, Gwin "gave people a way to find each other."[13]

27

Gwin thought up some revenue raisers and promoted them in *Mouth*— T-shirts declaring "Piss on Pity," bumper stickers warning "Pat My Head and I'll Break Your Legs," and sterling silver dog tags and posters of Lady

Liberty in a wheelchair. The wheelchair Liberty image, effective in its simplicity, became a lasting logo. The seated Lady, in black and white, graced *Mouth's* July–August 1992 cover—the "Independence Issue."

Gwin credited the World Institute on Disability, co-founded by Ed Roberts, for the wheelchair-bound Liberty, but its origin is unclear. Roberts and Gwin had been friends for years. He was among the leaders spotlighted in the pages of *Mouth*. Gwin dedicated six pages to him, plus two photographs, in the thirty-nine-page Independence issue. She recounted Roberts's background as a polio survivor hooked to a huge machine, his iron lung, which allowed him life, albeit without mobility. He had made a name for himself by insisting on a college education at the University of California, Berkeley. He became the first of the "Rolling Quads" who would gain entrance. Roberts was such a force behind the independent living movement that in 1976, California governor Jerry Brown appointed him to head the state agency that had previously labeled him too disabled to hold a job.

In the Independence issue, Gwin challenged the 375 centers for independent living nationwide to fight for improved vocational rehabilitation programs. She urged them to bolster their oversight of sheltered workshops and nursing homes to guard against abuses. She quoted Roberts's philosophy on seeking change, and it seemed to mirror Gwin's. "Too many teach us to suppress our anger, not use it. If anything, we're too passive," he said. "Anger is wonderful if you get energy out of it and *learn*."[1]

In 2007, another issue of *Mouth* featured a long interview with Roberts. The cover again featured Lady Liberty, but this time drawn by Melina Fatisiou-Cowan, an artist with spinal muscular atrophy. Unlike the black-and-white version of 1992, Fatisiou-Cowan's Liberty was printed in red and brown ink, sitting in a wheelchair without armrests. The flame she raised in her right hand was larger. The issue ran twelve years after Roberts's death. Gwin quoted him as praising ADAPT and saying, "We need to develop more militant leaders."[2]

Top ADAPT activists at the time viewed *Mouth* as a crusading publication and considered Gwin an influencer able to synthesize complex themes and ideas. "She really fueled the movement with her paper," said Stephanie Thomas, a national organizer for ADAPT from Texas and editor of the group's newsletter, *Incitement*. "She had a way of putting it in a simple way where it caught your attention." Gwin, she said, also encapsulated concepts in her signature bumper stickers and created slogans embraced by ADAPT supporters.[3]

Thomas acknowledged that *Mouth* could be tough on ADAPT, and even unfair, and pointed to Byzek's essay, saying she disagreed with its thesis. Sometimes Thomas got mad at Gwin and vice versa, but these sudden storms always blew over because each side saw the other as important to the overall mission of lifting up people with disabilities. Thomas recalled giving Gwin the mailing list for *Incitement* and asking Gwin for her list of subscribers. Instead Gwin gave her unusable data, making Thomas laugh to herself: Gwin was guarding her own territory. "She was a force of nature," Thomas said. "I was really glad I was exposed to it."

She saw Gwin at many ADAPT actions, acting as both a journalist and a participant. In May 1995, a few hundred people, many in wheelchairs, encircled then–House Speaker Newt Gingrich's apartment complex in Washington DC, Gwin joined with Thomas and other ADAPT activists to demand that the Republican leader get behind legislation known as MICASA, the Medicaid Community Attendant Services Act, which would allow Medicaid to fund services for persons with disabilities in their homes or in community-based settings so they would not be forced into an institution. Gwin herself was not walking well at the time and was getting around in a scooter.

Thomas and Gwin were among a contingent who had wanted to talk to Gingrich, but instead found themselves confronting a surrogate when the landlord of the apartment complex came out to meet them. "We went into the office and talked with the woman, and I have this strong memory of Lucy in this office with this woman and really bringing home what we were there about," Thomas said.

Gwin later wrote an article giving her own version of the events of that ADAPT action. She reported that five hundred activists visited various targets, making stops at the US Department of Health and Human Services to demand a meeting with Secretary Donna Shalala and at the Capitol, where they assumed they would meet with Gingrich. But he was a no-show. So, as Gwin put it, about a hundred peeled off and "invaded" the Speaker's residence, where they were told he was unavailable. The next day they got a meeting with Shalala and then returned to Gingrich's apartment building and surrounded it, barring entry and exit.[4]

Gwin also wrote about the third day's demonstration at Manor Care, Inc.'s, Maryland headquarters. ADAPT leaders met with the nursing home chain's top officer, arguing that 25 percent of Medicaid funding for nursing homes could be redirected to a national attendant care program. The group surrounded the office for most of the day, chanting, "Just Like a Nursing Home—You Can't Get Out."

The text was accompanied by pictures of uniformed officers taking away people in wheelchairs. In a sidebar that accompanied the coverage, Gwin published a nine-sentence quote from Frederick Douglass. It included this line: "Without struggle, there is no progress." During the Washington action, 110 protesters were arrested, Gwin reported. She called the activists "heroes." Two years later Gingrich introduced MICASA, but it was referred to committee without advancing.

28

In a *Mouth* column in late 1994, Gwin portrayed herself as overworked. She explained that she assembled each issue of the magazine with the assistance of designer/office manager/bulk mailer Bruce Faw, who had recently broken his arm. Each month, she had to dip into the magazine's modest bank balance—often less than $100. She received eight pounds of reader mail a day, she said, but wasn't complaining because she had the best job she'd ever held. It offered honest work, free of the fibbing that was common in her past life in advertising. She cherished the opportunity to learn and talk with real heroes. She asked for donors who might be able to help. "Bruce gets paid—not near what he's worth," she wrote. "I don't get paid at all. (SSDI supports me. I used to have some savings, but that's what got *Mouth* started and kept *Mouth* alive. It's gone now)."[1]

A few months later, in the summer 1995 issue, Gwin announced that Tom Olin, the preeminent photographer of the disability movement, had joined *Mouth* and Faw had moved on. The issue featured several pages of text, illustrated with Olin's pictures, about ADAPT leaders, including a Byzek interview with Stephanie Thomas and photos of ADAPT members protesting in Washington, DC, in May 1995. In the captions Gwin identified these people and praised many of them as "Action heroes" who had held fast in their wheelchairs despite the threat of arrest. They included Alan Holdsworth, aka Johnny Crescendo, a balladeer whose song "We Want What You've Got" became an anthem for the rights movement; "Julie," who had "wedged her way into the lobby of Newt Gingrich's apartment building and would not budge when security guards ganged up on her"; and a young man named "Weasel," who had "faced down a humongous cop on a humongous Harley in Newt's driveway."[2]

Around this time, freelance writer Fred Pelka interviewed Gwin about persons with disabilities and the attitude of the public toward them. "They want to kill us," she told him. She said she saw abortion and euthanasia as threats to Disability Nation. "I've had three abortions, and now that I'm past childbearing age I supposed I can say I'm against them."[3] Pelka said her apartment was like a bunker with piles of papers and clouds of cigarette smoke. He later worked on an encyclopedia of the movement, and Gwin helped him with a list of contacts. Eventually he compiled taped interviews of leaders of the movement and, in his book dealing with these oral histories, published several pages on Gwin and *Mouth*. According to Pelka, the magazine's coverage of disability rights had an impact well beyond its subscription base. "The mainstream media wasn't writing about this," he said.[4]

In summer 1995 Gwin announced in the magazine that she planned to send press packets to four hundred mainstream media members to "get the real disability issues" in front of journalists. "All of us would like to see the media cover disability issues without patting us on the head or confining us to a wheelchair the way they do," she wrote. But *Mouth* needed $2,000 for the media literacy campaign and didn't have $2 to spare. She asked for donations to help defray costs.[5]

The issue included a photo of police arresting Pennsylvania ADAPT leader and independent living center director Kathleen Kleinmann at the Washington action. Two officers have their hands on Kleinmann's wheelchair, and her wrists are handcuffed. Kleinmann met Gwin for the first time that May in the landlord's office at Gingrich's apartment complex. "I heard some conversation on my left side and I heard people saying 'Lucy.' I turned my head," recalled Kleinmann. "I said, 'Are you Lucy Gwin?' She looked me over for a half second. I said, 'I'm Kathleen.' It was exciting."[6] Kleinmann, from Washington, Pennsylvania, had talked with Gwin on the phone before, but this face-to-face meeting led to a closer relationship, which included Kleinmann submitting articles to *Mouth* and helping finance the publication through contracts with her center. In time Kleinmann assumed the role of treasurer of the nonprofit corporation Free Hand Press which Gwin set up as a holding company for the magazine.

Gwin came up with the corporate name because she didn't want anyone telling her what to do. Directors included friends, *Mouth* contributors, and associates, among them writer Billy Golfus, who for a time was president; Vikki Stefans, a rehab doctor in Arkansas who specialized in brain-injured patients; Michael Bailey, a Portland, Oregon, attorney whose daughter had Down syndrome; and Deidre Hammon, a Nevada activist with a daughter who used a wheelchair and a speaking device. All were fans of Gwin's. So was the lawyer for Free Hand Press, James A. Spall, a former Montana prosecutor. He had sustained debilitating brain damage when his car was struck by a semi-trailer truck four months before Gwin's own injury. He had been left comatose for months with eighty-seven stitches in his head. He was still recovering when he met Gwin. Both were active in their states' head injury associations, and Spall joined the board of the national association.

He incorporated Free Hand Press as a charity in Montana in 1991. It received tax-exempt status, meaning that donations could be tax deductible. He also helped Gwin deal with lawyers as she pursued government investigations of New Medico and credited her with foiling the chain. "She was one of the most competent people I know," Spall said.[7]

Vikki Stefans, who served as secretary of Free Hand Press, was drawn to Gwin because of *Mouth*'s scrutiny of rehabilitation services, and for assuming the role of watchdog over professionals, like her, who were supposed to help physically and mentally injured people and not try to run their lives. Gwin, she said, wanted to empower patients and get doctors and providers out of the habit of pushing the agenda. "She changed the mindset that it wasn't a top-down thing," said Stefans. She wrote some articles for the magazine and appreciated Gwin's ability to improve her essays.[8]

Hammon joined the board in 2007. More than twenty years later she remained grateful to Gwin for exhorting her to fight for equal education for her daughter Brianna. Gwin pushed her to stand up to authority. Without the force of *Mouth* and the guidance of Gwin, Hammon said, "I would have been a stupid parent. I would have gone along. Brianna would probably be in a sheltered workshop. I would have been another one of the dumbasses out there that doesn't understand disability."[9] When Hammon, a single mother of three, began reading *Mouth* in the early 1990s, its revolutionary tone scared her. But eventually it persuaded her to believe that she didn't have to accept what school administrators told her. "It finally liberated me," she wrote.[10] With her mother's backing, Brianna lodged a complaint in 1998 against the Washoe County School District, demanding that schools be designed to provide better access to buildings, washrooms, and water coolers. The complaint, filed under the Americans with Disabilities Act, was successful.

Hammon had become acquainted with Gwin years earlier, when she told Gwin about how Brianna, a student with cerebral palsy, had faced discrimination in her public school. Gwin had been outraged. That led to a piece in the May–June 2000 "Special Education" issue of *Mouth*. Hammon's article, "The Wooster High French Fry Conspiracy," recounted how Brianna had been followed by a teacher in the lunchroom.[11] The teacher wanted to make sure the girl ordered food the teacher considered appropriate, and not the corn dog and fried potatoes her mother allowed her to eat. "Lucy would hold me accountable. She would challenge me on every misguided notion I had which went toward the medical instead of the civil rights," Hammon recalled.[12] Hammon became a senior advocate for the Center for Self-Determination in Reno, and Brianna assumed the position of the center's librarian and international advocate.

29

Oregon lawyer Michael Bailey's involvement in *Mouth* and Free Hand Press came about because of his work with one of his daughters, Eleanor.

Her Down syndrome spurred him to become a statewide disability rights advocate and a member of national disability support groups, including ADAPT. As a result, around 2003 he went to a meeting in Virginia of government bureaucrats and was part of a panel that lauded the benefits of community living. He caused a stir by upbraiding a woman who was president of a pro-institution organization called Voice of the Retarded. Gwin caught wind of the encounter, and two weeks later Bailey's phone rang in Portland. She introduced herself as the editor of *Mouth* magazine and asked if she had found the Michael Bailey who had reprimanded the head of VOR. He said, "Yeah."

"Would you like to write for *Mouth*?" was the reply.[1]

Bailey took assignments, including serving as a correspondent for a lengthy report comparing a series of actions in 2005 in Washington, DC. One was an ADAPT protest against planned funding cuts to services for people with disabilities. Two other groups were also in the District for events. One was a coalition of professional developmental disabilities organizations, and the other was an antiwar coalition condemning the United States' involvement in Iraq. Bailey hailed the direct action of ADAPT and of the antiwar group, but he criticized the disabilities services professionals as having been too weak in their activism.

Bailey also wrote a couple of books about how to advocate for children with disabilities. Gwin edited the first one, on educational services. That one, Bailey said, outshines the other because of Gwin's touch. He described her editing style: "She wasn't mean. She was very clear: 'What the hell's this?'"

His young daughter Eleanor authored a piece for the March 2000 *Mouth*—an issue condemning patronizing caregivers. The article, "Eleanor Helps Herself," included her photo. Eleanor's story was from her own journal entries at age eleven attending a convention of TASH. Eleanor revealed that she had figured out that she had something called Down syndrome and had tried to wash it away during baths or cover it with sunscreen and hair spray. "I got my name from Eleanor Roosevelt," she told *Mouth* readers. "Lots of bad things happened in her life. I have read all about her. She was a leader."[2] Eleanor's story "was reprinted by every Down syndrome organization on earth. It made Eleanor a celebrity," Bailey said. She was invited to speak across the country and gave the keynote address at a National Down Syndrome Association meeting.

Gwin never forgot her and sent her cards and gifts for years. At first she had asked Bailey if it would be all right to mail such personal items to Eleanor. She had tried to send gifts to her own grandkids, she confided to Bailey, but they were returned unopened. "She told me that several times," Bailey said.

Bailey and his family visited Gwin at the new Mouth House in Topeka and they hosted her in Oregon. She enjoyed spending time with Bailey's children and the children of other disability leaders she came to know, Bailey said.

As well as she got along with other people's children, she was unable to reconnect with her own. For a spell, her daughter Christine stayed in touch as a young woman, sometimes writing and receiving calls from her mother. She accepted a briefcase Gwin sent her in 1987 and wrote a thank you note, addressing her mother as Lucy.[3] But Gwin's older daughter, Tracy, kept her distance. The sisters had lived with their father for much of their childhood. When he remarried, they became part of a bigger family with a stepmother and siblings. Then they married and had children themselves. It pained Gwin that she could not be part of their lives.

According to Peter Walker, a childhood friend of Tracy's, the wedge between mother and daughter came about when Tracy took a strong interest in Christianity in the mid-1970s. The teen was intrigued by the rock opera *Jesus Christ Superstar*, he said, and began associating with fundamentalist Christians. "Lucy had such strong convictions, she seemed to be willing to burn her bridges with her own daughter [over] what she considered a poor choice . . . Her whole being was opposed to the regimented conformity of religion," said Walker.[4] At the time, Tracy was living with Gwin at 20 Thayer Street in Rochester, not far from the residence that would eventually become the Mouth House. Mother and daughter had shouting matches, said Walker, who often visited the apartment with his father, Ernie Walker, Gwin's former lover.

Tracy was a near straight-A student and had an independent streak. "Ironically, she was like her mother, very passionate, very smart, but they ended up locking horns," Walker recalled. He described Gwin as drama-prone and given to exhibiting extreme highs and lows. She was tender toward him, however, and they stayed in touch throughout her life, even after his father died.

According to Tracy Hanes, Peter Walker's version of her story isn't on target.[5] She said the break with her mother didn't erupt until after the teen moved back to Illinois to live with her father and his family. She met a fellow in college and got married in November 1979, two months before she turned nineteen. She invited her mother to the wedding and asked her to bring Verna, who didn't drive. Gwin wouldn't do it, Hanes said, because it was too difficult for her to be around her ex-husband. Hanes denied that she had a religious conversion, though the family did attend a local church, and she was married in that same church, where her husband was a member of the congregation.

Hanes believed that her mother, whom she tended to refer to as Lucy, not Mom, loved her in her own way but wasn't cut out for motherhood. That was why Gwin took off when her daughters were toddlers. Gwin originally had custody, but in the mid-1960s, after finding the girls unattended, their father successfully petitioned to have them come live with him. Seven years later, when he and his second wife were having difficulties, he arranged for the sisters to live temporarily with Gwin in Chicago. "We didn't even remember we had another mother," Hanes said.

Gwin was nervous at first. She hadn't spent time with the girls in seven years. "I was frightened—or should I say apprehensive," she wrote to a friend in June 1972. "But now I'm just thrilled." She had thought that her biological ties had vanished but "fell in love all over again as soon as I saw the backs of their necks." Gwin boasted about how beautiful, bright, energetic, and talkative they were. She described Tracy as a natural ad writer who'd made a poster that asked, "If you can't eat crows, why shoot them?" As for "Crickie," she was more self-indulgent, emotional, and artsy—a romantic. Gwin planned to sit them down for their first conversation about sex, because they were spending time at her Dodgeville farm and witnessing copulating pigs, goats, sheep, cows, and chickens.[6]

The bad news, Gwin confided, was that the return of the girls had scared off Mike London. "Being the father to 2 pre-teeners wasn't in his contract," Gwin wrote. "After 24 hours with them (and they're LOVELY,

QUIET, POLITE, INDUSTRIOUS, INTERESTING, OBEDIENT kids)
he started packing." Gwin could not predict how long the children would
be with her. But London didn't stay away for long.[7]

After six months with Gwin, the girls were invited to return to their
father's home in Decatur. Christine chose to go back. Tracy preferred the
freedom of living with her mother and remained with Gwin for the next
seven years. In Decatur, "we had a lot more rules, couldn't move everywhere
we wanted, had to wear dresses," Hanes said.

After her high school graduation in 1978, Tracy went back to Illinois,
and she and her sister didn't see Gwin until Verna's funeral in 1989. Gwin
explained to a friend that she avoided Tracy's wedding for two key reasons:
"Too poor. Also too transparently exasperated." She wrote that Tracy "longs
for a perfect happy family. So did I at that age." She predicted that her
daughter had a better chance at succeeding. Gwin added she did not fear
"grandmotherhood . . . It's got to be an improvement over motherhood!?!"[8]

Christine traveled to Rochester once to visit her mother in the
hospital after the accident. Her sister listened to the doctors, Hanes said,
and tried to take care of some bills to help Gwin. "She got a tongue-lashing
for it," according to Hanes.

Gwin adapted to the estrangement from her daughters but did try
to mend her relationships, particularly with her younger daughter. Gwin
looked forward to seeing them at Verna's funeral, but whatever goodwill
was created in that reunion didn't overcome the problems in their relationships. She wrote to Christine in 1990 after her head injury and asked
her to forgive her for her past behavior. "I miss you. I care about you," she
wrote. "I said and did a lot of terrible things. I'm very sorry. And I spend
every day, believe me, being more unselfish than the day before. Telling
the truth, absolutely, no matter what." She asked Christine to give a secret
kiss to Tracy and her family. "I miss you all."[9]

The overture failed. A decade later, Gwin revealed the depth of the
disaffection as well as her aptitude for harshness. In a letter to the editor
of the disability movement magazine *Ragged Edge,* she criticized the idea
of placing unwanted children with disabilities in institutions rather than
putting them up for adoption. She had a seventy-pound dog named Homey,
she wrote, that she had brought home from a shelter and was now putting
up for adoption because of the hound's chronic misbehavior. Reacting to

a story about a family that had given up on their son, who needed twenty hours a day of services, Gwin asked, "If they didn't want him anymore, did adoption cross their minds?"[10]

Then she parenthetically noted that she had "raised two lovely and talented little girls who grew up to be Republicans. One of them is a born-again-Christian-home-schooling life insurance broker, the other a suburbanite-Aryan-nation-loving personnel director for a nuclear power plant. They are, in short, everything I'm not. If I'd known how they were going to turn out, I would have put them up for adoption for sure."[11]

PART FOUR

When you're born you get a ticket for the freak show. Some of us get to sit and watch the freaks and describe them; some of us are in the rings and we are the freaks; and others of us want to fix the freaks.
—*George Carlin*

30

A few publications covered the disability rights movement before *Mouth* came onto the scene, most notably Mary Johnson's *Disability Rag,* which was renamed *Ragged Edge.* Gwin and Johnson saw themselves as allies and competitors. Johnson's magazine used some of the same contributors Gwin used, but their work was packaged in a conventional, factual manner in "the *Rag*" and in a more sensational style in the format Gwin delivered.

Gwin sought collaborations with Johnson, and when the *Rag*'s managing editor, Sharon Kutz-Mellem, planned to step down, Gwin wrote to Kutz-Mellem about options going forward, perhaps even a merger. In an August 13, 1991, letter, Gwin told her: "The world needs two bodacious non-stop rowdy rags. Friends who subscribe to both tell me: 'They're DIFFERENT.'"[1]

"*Mouth* is an *underground magazine* focused on the whole foggin' rehab system, inside & out, private & government," Gwin wrote. "I won't stop mouthing off until that's done. As I said a few months back. Client must become Customer . . . *Rag*, it seems to me, is more of a news magazine. Journalism, not propaganda. Respectable in the best sense. The world needs both."

Readers did see a difference. Josie Byzek, who wrote for both, considered *Mouth* much more of an organ for hardcore disability rights advocates. ADAPT leader Mike Oxford, who ran an independent living center in Topeka for years, described Johnson as taking the typical journalist's objective third-person approach to the news, whereas Gwin traded in subjective first-person accounts. "Lucy's [magazine] wasn't objective," Oxford said. *Mouth* covered the "people's perspective, and they were people who were hacked off." Gwin helped frame the purpose of the movement and helped give persons with disabilities "independence and agency."[2]

According to Johnson, anyone who knew her and knew Gwin could tell which magazine was put out by which editor. She said the *Rag* tried to report the news straight. Her husband had been a journalist with the Louisville *Courier-Journal,* and that influenced her practice. Gwin, she said, had no interest in that approach and tried to persuade Johnson to get punchier. "She was pushing people, she was marketing, she was organizing. Lucy was louder than I was. I always had this thing about objectivity: both sides," Johnson said. "I felt if I wrote things the way she wanted me to write, the *Rag* would lose its credibility." Gwin also got upset with her for not joining demonstrations. "She wanted me to be there, and I was very uncomfortable with that," Johnson said. "I frustrated Lucy and Lucy irritated me." She respected Gwin but found her intimidating.[3]

Once when Gwin was visiting family in the Louisville area, she contacted Johnson and asked to meet at the offices of the *Rag*. Johnson couldn't recall the year, but she remembered her anxiety. She feared a face-to-face encounter because Gwin often seemed to be upset and lecturing. Johnson called Tom Olin, whom she had known for years. He assured Johnson that Gwin wasn't on the attack. Still, "Lucy was unpredictable, whereas I am not," said Johnson.

The visit went well, and on the drive to Johnson's home, Gwin pointed out her maternal grandmother's house a few blocks away. In November 1989 Gwin jotted down her childhood memories of "Gomie's" rooming house—the gas fire in the bathroom, the poured stone steps with built-in pots for geraniums, the steep stairs leading to a room with a huge "invalid" in bed wearing ballerina slippers. Gomie, she said, served as a model for her concept of an invalid. "I won't have that life!" Gwin wrote. "(Though I've certainly flirted with it, off and on.)" In the journal entry, Gwin remembered how her mother and Gomie fought over her soul. Gwin was the battleground, the blood and lumps left over after the fight. "No one would accuse me of being a nice person," she summed up.[4] Johnson didn't recall Gwin sharing personal information.

Gwin stayed in touch with Johnson and even raised the idea of publishing joint issues and sharing subscriber lists. The *Rag*, which started almost a decade before *Mouth*, ceased printing in 2005. Johnson admired Gwin's drive. Gwin, said Kutz-Mellem, took movement coverage to another level. The former *Rag* editor, who left in 1992 to enter the ministry, said Gwin reached people with her rawness, her spunkiness, her "piss and vinegar," adding, "She was sort of the next generation and we were like the grandmothers."[5]

31

Gwin used to say that she started her magazine with credit cards issued to her when she was still writing copy for ad agencies, a time when her salary afforded a middle-class lifestyle and even a mink coat if she wished. She told people she lived well selling lies. In keynote speeches at conferences on independent living, she said she had awakened to reality thanks to her head injury. It had opened her eyes to the perils of life in nursing homes and institutions and had shown her how such places took hostages for money. She pledged to dedicate herself to telling these truths.

She became a well-known figure in the disability community, consulting with and interviewing leaders—Justin Dart Jr., Wade Blank (a founder of ADAPT), Ed Roberts, and others. "I'm proud to say that I have personally seen to Ed's bowel program," she wrote in a speech in 1994 for the Virginia Council for Independent Living conference.[1]

In 1996 she published *Mouth*'s four-part mission statement, which pledged, "first and foremost, to promote the freedoms of all people with disabilities." She promised to print truthful and factual accounts, to assist like-minded entities, and to investigate and bring to public awareness those who would undermine the rights of people with disabilities.[2] More than two decades earlier, Gwin had read another magazine from which she borrowed concepts for her own. She credited that publication, *Madness Network News*, for inspiring her format and style. Joel Frank had subscribed to it and sometimes provided art for its pages. Gwin considered *Madness Network News* to be a voice for people with histories of mental health problems and a watchdog on the psychiatric industry.[3] The logo of the magazine was a graphic of a wild-haired person with a wide-open mouth and a raised clenched fist, breaking free of a straitjacket. The magazine described itself as a quarterly journal "of the psychiatric inmates/anti-psychiatry movement." Its pages contained patients' first-person stories as well as articles about demonstrations outside psychiatric centers and VA hospitals. The magazine's writers condemned many methods of psychiatric treatment, with particular disdain for electroshock and drug therapies used by "pro-shock shrinks" and "nut doctors."[4] Issue number 6 of Gwin's magazine featured a cover illustration from *Madness Network News*, which Gwin identified as "an important human rights magazine of the Seventies." The illustration showed six people in a gerbil cage with an insurance bill of $1,067 per client.[5]

Mouth gained attention for its own illustrations. Bruce Faw's graphic design for the cover of the November–December 1994 issue won an award from the Art Directors Club of New York. The cover showed an enlarged dollar bill over which lay "one disabled dollar" with a goofy Liberty image and a motto reading, "In doG We Trust." In easy-to-follow graphics, the issue tracked the trail of money extracted from patients and their care, particularly public dollars. Two years later, the *Utne Reader* gave *Mouth* its Alternative Press Award in the "special interest" category. In announcing the honor, *Utne*'s editor, Hugh Delehanty, informed Gwin that she deserved recognition for "the consistent excellence of your publication." Gwin returned the award to the Minneapolis-based magazine, declaring that civil rights was not "special."[6]

Gwin edited her magazine for an audience she thought of as survivors, people she wanted treated as customers. In 1993 she opened her pages to John McKnight, a Northwestern University professor and former federal bureaucrat. She revered his research on how institutions seek to control care. McKnight had entered academia by way of neighborhood organizing. He was also a top officer of the Illinois American Civil Liberties Union and a manager for federal civil rights agencies. His book *The Careless Society* was critical of social service agencies. Its themes appealed to Gwin, who denounced professional caregivers in her magazine.

Gwin contacted McKnight and asked if she could publish his work. He was amazed that she had discovered his writings. "Of the voices, hers was the most urgent, most confrontational, most vivid about things that were wrong," McKnight said. "There were a significant number of people who were very tough, tell-it-like-it-is advocates, but she was the only one who put it on paper."[7] His debut in *Mouth* came by way of an interview with Billy Golfus headlined "Care and Control." The article featured a pullout quote: "Everything comes at you and says to you that what's important about you is what you aren't. And that disables people."[8]

That same issue reprinted an official statement from Justin Dart Jr., then chairman of the President's Committee on Employment of People with Disabilities, on the tragic death of Wade Blank. Blank, a disability rights leader from Denver and a founder of ADAPT, drowned in the surf at Todos Santos, Mexico, in a vain attempt to save his eight-year-old son, Lincoln. "Unlike others who participated in the sixties revolution for a rational society, Wade did not give up the struggle," Dart wrote.[9]

Also remarkable about that 1993 issue was an essay by Bill Bolte, "Final Care, Final Control," which decried assisted suicide, its well-known advocate Dr. Jack Kevorkian, and the "right to die" lobby.[10] It was the first time Gwin dipped into the subject, and it would become another constant theme of her magazine. It became her Liberty torch in a crusade to defend the powerless from the powerful. The cause would eventually lead her to the steps of the US Supreme Court.

In addition to *Mouth*, Free Hand Press produced "You Choose," a grouping of elegant publications for lobbying and educating the public about the costs of nursing home care compared with services from attendants in the community. For the 1995 project, Gwin researched, collected data, and created content for the photo-rich red-white-and-blue packets and pamphlets. With graphs and short information boxes, the "You Choose" packages told the story of the cost to taxpayers of putting people with disabilities in institutions. The packets were the kind that a high-end public relations firm might assemble, distilling facts and figures into easy-to-digest data with bite-sized statements and accompanying pictures. The bottom-line message: costs are more than four times greater for institutional care than for the personal care option. Gwin estimated that ten thousand advocates used the material to push for changes in state and federal long-term care policies. Here Gwin was using her advertising skills in a new genre—comprehensive advocacy handouts.

Gwin urged activists to use the packets in meetings with legislators and to help educate the press on the wisdom of deinstitutionalization. In binder and in booklet form, the materials were the first in a series of training manuals, guides, and lobbying aids created by Free Hand Press. Other packets included an "Organizers' Tool Kit" to help people assemble teams of activists, and "The Hearts & Minds Project," which came with a

CD containing PowerPoint presentations explaining bigotry and disability rights along with tips on how to get on the agendas of meetings of those without disabilities. Gwin called it "disability rights karaoke," adding, "Remember you're doing this for their own good."[11]

32

Gwin's ability to frame issues and make simple and pointed arguments was on full display in the winter of 1996–97, when she launched an ambitious nationwide effort to combat what she viewed as a major threat to Disability Nation: doctor-assisted suicide. She took the lead, at substantial expense to *Mouth*'s budget, in organizing one of the most visible demonstrations in disability rights history. About five hundred people marched in the rally she marshaled, many on crutches or in wheelchairs. They confronted one hundred proponents of assisted suicide outside the US Supreme Court. Working with Diane Coleman, chief executive officer of the disability rights group Not Dead Yet, Gwin planned the event for months. She created a giant banner, using a thriller font and hot-pink background, as well as other eye-catching displays and logos for the protest. She had been promoting the January event in *Mouth* and using the magazine's headquarters and telephone number for calls and letters from interested activists and participants. "Her advertising skills definitely got into her advocacy in a big way," Coleman recalled.[1]

Coleman had met Gwin years earlier and in 1993 invited her and a few other activists to her apartment in a schoolhouse in Tennessee to talk about the "Kevorkian problem." Gwin was keen on countering "right to die" with "right to live" and began portraying Dr. Jack Kevorkian as the enemy, a vile, warped executioner, for helping people with disabilities take lethal doses of medication. By early 1997, when the Supreme Court met to consider the constitutionality of bans on doctor-assisted suicide, Gwin was already working at a fever pitch. The *Mouth* staff had called and faxed people all over the country to plan the protest, and Gwin enlisted former US surgeon general C. Everett Koop, who had worked in the

Reagan administration, to march with the Not Dead Yet group. Justin Dart Jr. also took part.

Gwin had been likening assisted suicide to the Nazis' death trains. When the hearing date at the Supreme Court was set for January 8, 1997, she sounded the alert. She published a special eight-page "Emergency Edition" of *Mouth* on December 12, 1996, calling on readers to join its National Heroes Project and take part in the vigil outside the court. She envisioned twenty thousand protesters showing up, chanting "We Want to Live!"

At the event, Gwin did some live radio spots with stations in Rochester to discuss the importance of the court hearing and provide dispatches on the protest. "Most of the activism was done well before the rally to organize and coordinate everything," noted Joe Ehman.[2] Gwin wrote commentary pieces, including one op-ed that ran under her byline over the Knight Ridder/Tribune News Service. Blasting "the great American mercy-killing craze," the piece was published in multiple newspapers on the day of the Supreme Court hearing. The *Atlanta Constitution* ran it under the headline "Killing Us with 'Kindness.'" She also talked Evan Kemp, President George H. W. Bush's chairman of the Equal Employment Opportunity Commission, into writing an op-ed for the *Washington Post* condemning assisted suicide. Kemp had recently had a stroke, so the essay was actually written by his wife, Janine Bertram Kemp, and Gwin. It was published on the day of the Supreme Court hearing, Bertram Kemp recalled, noting that Justice David Souter referred to the commentary during the justices' discussion.[3] The Washington bureau of Knight-Ridder covered the protest in a story that ran in numerous papers. The reporter described Gwin, wearing a bright red coat and blowing a plume of smoke in the frigid air, saying, "I'm not going to die for Jack Kevorkian or anybody just because they think I'm not pretty to look at." Others quoted were Evan Kemp and Clark Goodrich, a protester from Grand Rapids, Michigan.[4]

Gwin, Ehman, and Olin staffed the rally. The evening before they left Rochester in a rented van, Gwin saw something unusual in the trees in front of the Mouth House. Branches were filled with crows, flapping and cawing in "solemn, croaky, crowtalk," Gwin wrote. "Crows do not fly at night. Crows don't even breathe loud after dark. That's when high-flying owls hear crow hearts beating and swoop right down." The scene was a sign, she declared, a good one. It reminded her of a time eleven years earlier when she'd had surgery and a crow landed on her car door and made noises that surely meant that everything was going to be all right.[5]

Protesters at the rally were chilled by the wind and cold of the nation's capital in winter. Gwin stood out in her scarlet coat as she hugged participants, recalled Nadina LaSpina, an activist from New York City who had responded to Gwin's call to join and helped arrange a caravan of a few school buses filled with activists coming to the protest. Jennifer Burnett, a *Mouth* writer from Pennsylvania, recalled people ducking into an alley to warm themselves at a trash can fire. Burnett made trips to a coffee shop for hot drinks. Gwin, she said, was antagonistic toward participants in the Kevorkian camp. She described Gwin yelling at them. "I remember being uncomfortable with it," Burnett said. "She was very, very passionate." Burnett had mixed feelings about the case because she knew persons with disabilities who desired the option of dying to end chronic pain and needed a physician's help if they chose to do so.[6]

A remarkable thing happened in Washington: mass coverage. A photograph in the next issue of *Mouth* shows a slim Gwin smiling like a schoolgirl, holding up the front page of the January 9 *USA Today*. The lead story in the national newspaper was about the Supreme Court case. It featured a picture of, as Gwin put it, "angry cripples."[7] Mainstream media had recognized the movement. "She was so proud of it," Burnett said. "It was a complete success in her view." Justin Dart Jr. agreed, calling Gwin's work a "historic contribution."[8] He sent Gwin a note four days after the event telling her, "You are great! Congratulations on the great media coverage you so well managed to get!"[9]

33

As Gwin was directing her energy toward "right to die" challenges, she also resumed her love life. In the January–March 1997 issue of *Mouth*, she told her readers that she hadn't had a boyfriend for seven years but had become attracted to a younger man who used a wheelchair. An ADAPT activist from Michigan, "Weasel" had impressed Gwin when he had stood up to a police officer in the driveway of Newt Gingrich's apartment complex two years earlier. The cop, Gwin wrote in *Mouth*, was revving his Harley-Davidson and bumping it against Weasel's power chair. Despite being as "crushable as a pop can," Weasel refused to budge. "That boy and that scene grabbed my heart by the roots," Gwin confessed. She disclosed their budding relationship by describing Weasel stroking her arm with his mouth stick. She revealed she spent the night before the Not Dead Yet march with him but said she would have to hold off on more information about their physical relationship unless she produced a "People Are Still Having Sex" issue of the magazine.[1]

According to Clark "Weasel" Goodrich, he had an eighteen-month affair with Gwin.[2] They began corresponding and calling after the motorcycle cop incident. She told him she'd shed about eighty pounds to make herself more attractive. The relationship became physical in the hotel where they were staying on January 7, 1997, the night before the Supreme Court rally Gwin had organized. He was twenty-five; she had turned fifty-four two days earlier. She praised his writing and gave him attention. During their affair, Gwin drove to his apartment in Michigan three or four times from Rochester for long weekends. And they would sometimes meet at ADAPT actions. He said Gwin made him feel the most confident he has ever felt with a woman. He received numerous love notes and postcards from Gwin, some that simply had a heart and an L written on them.

The relationship broke down, he said, because Gwin became too controlling. Once she embarrassed him at a Chinese restaurant at a table they were sharing with a group of ADAPT activists. She announced how she'd had great sex the previous day, making it clear that she was referring to a romp with Goodrich. That was followed by her growing jealous of a female aide who worked for Goodrich for years. A drive back from an ADAPT action with Gwin and the aide was so tense that he thought Gwin might do something rash before they got to Michigan. The next morning, he said, he split up with her.

Still, he remembers Gwin fondly as generous, fun, and brilliant. She loved and talked to birds and had mused that she might come back to life as one. If he had "any claim to fame," said Goodrich, a freelance editor, "it was that I was with Lucy Gwin for a year and half."

In handwritten notes in the accounts books of Free Hand Press, where Gwin would jot down important events, she recorded some of her activities in 1996 as "Not Dead Yet full time," "Joe works his butt off," and "I fell in love—personally—in here somewhere." In 1997 she recorded going to an ADAPT action in Washington, followed by "return to Michigan, dumpola."[3] Gwin wrote about the end of the affair in the fall issue of *Mouth* in such detail that there was no doubt about how she felt—"like a woman whose tits have just been ripped off her chest."[4] In a letter to Weasel warning him not to cross her path at the ADAPT action in 1998, she told him she was so angry at him for the breakup that she wished he were dead. "I don't feel that toward the guy who raped me. Him, I fear. You, I hate."[5]

Her disclosures about intimacy with Weasel weren't the first time Gwin referred in the magazine to the subject of sexuality among people with disabilities. The front page of the May–June 1994 issue, called "The Trouble with Sex," featured a pair of nude women locked in an embrace in a wheelchair. Among the articles in that issue were autobiographical essays—such as "Queen of the Girls"—in which the writers detailed sexual encounters. Gwin wrote about her affair with a nineteen-year-old during her stay at the New Medico rehab center. Billy Golfus's piece was head-lined "Sex and the Single Gimp." The edition triggered numerous letters to the editor in subsequent issues, many of them positive, some of them not. One reader from North Carolina said she was writing to cancel her subscription. A married woman who'd been in a wheelchair for thirty-three years said she was stopping the "rotten, off-color magazine" at once. Some criticized Golfus for betraying his partner's privacy, while another said she had cried tears of affirmation. A writer from Honolulu confessed that after sixty years of living in a crippled body, *Mouth*'s "Sex" issue "brought back vivid memories of moments in my life that were sensual, sexual, and erotic." A reader from Berkeley, California, wrote, "Sex . . . does not end because of being a crip." A photograph of a nude woman—a self-portrait by the blind photographer Flo Fox—accompanied the Golfus piece. Fox, arms above her head, gazes at her reflection in a mirror.

On the cover of the January–February 1996 *Mouth*, called "Waking Up," Gwin published a blurred sketch of a nude woman sitting up in bed like someone waking from a dream. The issue included vignettes from seven people about their being called to the movement. One writer is Goodrich, another is Gwin, and a third is Ehman. "It's amazing seeing the power of all the crips coming together," Goodrich wrote.[6]

34

Mouth branched into hard-hitting journalism. It published its most ambitious package in the March–April 1998 magazine. Called "Justice Undone," the issue was dominated by the findings of its five-month investigation of the US Department of Justice's Disability Rights Section and its enforcement of the Americans with Disabilities Act. Four reporters were credited, including Gwin and Mary Johnson of *Ragged Edge*. Much of the report was based on whistleblower leaks. It also included data, documents, and confrontational interviews with DOJ administrators. It held Clinton administration officials accountable for having litigated just one prosecution alleging violations of the ADA in the five years sincetaking office. Gwin quoted a retired DOJ lawyer who said on the record that the department was afraid of pushing powerful people around. Gwin's team found thirty-five ADA cases that had been filed. Just three had been initiated by the DOJ, and only one had gone to trial. Gwin also reported that although the DOJ's own Disability Rights Section employed twenty people with disabilities, the department's offices were not ADA-compliant.

In the article, Gwin took aim at John Wodatch, a lawyer for the federal government who had helped write key statutes and regulations on disability rights. Yet as head of the Disability Rights Section, he had not cracked down hard enough on violators to suit Gwin and other activists. When *Mouth* singled him out for weak enforcement, "it was a shock, because I saw myself then, and I still do, as a disability rights advocate," said Wodatch more than two decades after the article appeared, "but I also know that I work for the government, and we thought we were doing a vigorous job . . . [T]hat does not mean that we are moving fast enough for everyone." The story forced him to assess his performance, and he made sure his office secured a *Mouth* subscription to diversify feedback beyond the established organizations. "This was a different voice and a different format, grittier . . . a little sensational," Wodatch said.[1]

In an article for the summer 1998 issue of *Curio*, an arts and culture magazine for which Gwin wrote sometimes, she characterized *Mouth*'s DOJ exposé as a "scoop" by amateurs. "Nobody here knows much about professional journalism," she wrote. "None of us can even put high school reporting on our c.v."[2] The story in *Curio* was accompanied by Tom Olin's "Capitol crawl" photo. It portrayed the rights struggle in a visceral way, showing ADAPT activists who had shed their crutches and wheelchairs pushing themselves up the steps of the US Capitol in their fight for passage of the ADA on March 12, 1990.

Four months later, Olin would be back with his camera to photograph President George H. W. Bush signing the ADA into law. Evan Kemp, head of the EEOC, and Justin Dart Jr. sat in their wheelchairs on either side of the president. Kemp and Dart became financial backers of *Mouth*, and Kemp's wife, Janine Bertram Kemp, became a writer for the magazine.

A story in the magazine's DOJ investigative package featured Sara Kaltenborn, a DOJ lawyer who retired in frustration in 1996. She does not recall being interviewed by Gwin or appearing in *Mouth*. But twenty-two years after being quoted by Gwin criticizing her former employer, she reiterated almost word for word what Gwin reported—that the department wouldn't enforce the ADA and would not pick fights with big organizations or businesses.[3] *Mouth* also quoted DOJ administrators, giving them the opportunity to respond to the failure to prosecute. One said the department preferred to settle rather than sue.

35

After twenty-three years in Rochester, Gwin decided to move. She had developed a bond with Mike "Mo" Oxford, the director of the Topeka independent living center. He was a veteran ADAPT leader with a flair for spectacular activism. He helped put together national actions and had staged protests at the Kansas state capitol. Once, when two state legislators were holding up a vote on expanding public health care for 150,000 people with disabilities, he organized a team to drop 150,000 pieces of mail from the upper level of the statehouse's airy rotunda. They also unfurled a banner covered in bloody handprints and demonstrated outside the homes of Kansas lawmakers.

Oxford helped arrange Gwin's relocation from New York, providing some financing and contracts for writing and editing. Gwin was excited to be associated with what she considered a model center and a take-charge activist. The Topeka Independent Living Resource Center was headquartered in a historic building built a century earlier by a Kansas governor. With big rooms, some still containing bank vaults, the landmark offered plenty of space for people in wheelchairs and for storing motorized wheelchairs and other accessories collected and refurbished to be handed out to those in need. Oxford's independent living center was on *Mouth*'s "bestest" list because it was succeeding in providing services to people with disabilities while fighting to get more of them free of institutions.

Joe Maurer helped Gwin pack in Rochester, and she and Olin drove away in late 1998. In Topeka, Kevin Siek helped find a ranch house outside of town to become the new headquarters of *Mouth*. Gwin lived on the first floor and Olin took the basement. According to Gwin, 22,000 pounds of mess had to be moved from Rochester to Kansas. "We know that Topeka is going to make a great home town for *Mouth*," she told readers.[1]

Oxford was one of her heroes. She wrote to Justin Dart Jr. in May 1998 that Dart and Oxford were "the two leaders I would follow into the fire."[2] Oxford was also among a group of leaders who helped Gwin dig out from $44,000 in debt from *Mouth*'s Not Dead Yet initiatives. In June 1998, Oxford, Dart, ADAPT leader Bob Kafka, Not Dead Yet's Diane Coleman, and Janine Bertram Kemp lent their names to a three-page form letter used to raise funds for Gwin. They urged people to send money to the magazine. Otherwise, the letter warned, the latest issue, which came out in May, would be the last: "We can't let that happen. It is hard hitting, thought provoking, a true disability rights magazine that never pulls its punches." The letter writers said that *Mouth*'s staff had dropped everything to push for the Supreme Court rally, a protest that ended up on the front pages of 370 newspapers nationwide. "Our voices were heard," the letter stated. "Thousands of lives were saved because the MOUTH saw the emergency and the opportunity, and acted fast." But Olin and Gwin had covered expenses with their credit cards and now didn't have the funds to make payments. "We owe MOUTH a debt we can never repay. But we must try," the letter said in a boldfaced, underlined appeal.[3]

The move made Gwin happy. She extolled the "free" territory of Kansas, which had been the home of the antislavery zealot John Brown. He had moved to the Sunflower State from New York in the 1850s, a few years before his bloody takeover of the federal arsenal in Harpers Ferry, Virginia. For her part, Gwin made sure the covers of *Mouth* featured African Americans, some with disabilities. One published in 1999, after the move to Kansas, featured a young man in a wheelchair. Another in 2002 showed a small girl with ankle braces sitting on a curb. Another in 2004 showed a man in a T-shirt declaring "Expect the Respect." A 2003 cover displayed an Olin portrait of a boy, the grandson of Justin Dart Jr., and in 2005 a cover in blue and white featured a photo by Olin of Dana Washington, granddaughter of the Dart, speaking at the 2004 Disability Pride Parade. Inside, the magazine quoted the Black woman: "Our pride and our love for one another are, in the end, what will assure us victory in our struggle to overcome."[4]

36

In Topeka, Gwin had a smaller social network—especially after Olin moved out in 1999.

An itinerant photographer known for living in an aged bus for much of his life, Olin often roomed with leaders of the movement and would end up changing addresses every few seasons. After nearly five years with Gwin, he had an opportunity to relocate to Janine Bertram Kemp's home in Washington, DC. She had become a widow in 1997, when Evan Kemp Jr. died at age sixty, seven years after he and Dart ushered in the ADA in the momentous bill signing on the lawn of the White House. Bertram Kemp became an ADAPT media specialist and had been writing for *Mouth* and other publications while her husband headed the Equal Employment

Opportunity Commission. She had helped Gwin and Olin organize for the 1997 Not Dead Yet rally and had spent much of her life devoted to social justice issues after a revolutionary youth that included a prison stint for crimes committed as a member of a violent anti-government group. After her husband's passing, Bertram Kemp had ample room for Olin, and he would have more photography opportunities in Washington.

When Bertram Kemp went to Topeka to help Olin pack, Gwin was in a foul mood. She promised to control her anger but cursed at her and "exploded," calling her a "sellout."[1] But, as was her style, Gwin eventually calmed down in a few days and resumed a working relationship with both Olin and Bertram Kemp.

For years, Gwin kept business records and notes in a red accounting book. Gwin's notes for 1999 provide fragments of the chronology: "Tom gave 3 mos notice 1/28/99," "I'm trapped," "LONESOME!" "Tom packing," "Tom gone," and "real quiet here." Besides the usual recording of incoming mail, money receipts, milestones, and observations, she noted that she was dealing with asthma. She applauded the issues of the magazine that came out that year, numbers 52 and 54 in particular. She also recorded the number of fish still alive in her backyard goldfish pond. By June she was in a better humor because of breaking news: "We won Olmstead!"[2]

If Gwin needed a pick-me-up, the Supreme Court decision in the case of *Olmstead v. L.C.* was better than hitting the Kansas lottery. The case referred to Tommy Olmstead, commissioner of Georgia's Department of Human Resources, who had been sued by two women with disabilities over housing discrimination. In her magazine, Gwin painted Olmstead as a buffoon. The case had come before the high court at the start of the year, and each step was detailed in *Mouth*. Indeed, the cover of the March–April 1999 issue featured a graphic of a man in a judge's robe holding up a gavel. Under the banner headline "Judgment Day," Gwin wrote, "Coming soon. Just weeks from now, the United States Supreme Court will determine if states have the right to lock you away for the crime of having a disability." Gwin wrote an autobiographical essay about being held in the New Medico "home," revealing, "I do not sleep well in my own bed, for fear that I will awaken in that place."[3]

The *Olmstead* case dealt specifically with whether public agencies were required to provide for people with disabilities to live in the community if they chose to remain at home instead of being treated or cared for in an institution. In a six-to-three ruling, the justices determined that "undue institutionalization" was a form of discrimination in violation of the ADA. "Unjustified placement or retention of persons in institutions severely limits their exposure to the outside community," the court stated. Gwin was overjoyed with the decision, and it mobilized her. Partnering with *Ragged Edge* and others, she launched a project to get every state to enforce the decision. She formed a coalition called the Freedom Clearinghouse, intent on keeping the pressure on governments to recognize and honor the watershed Supreme Court ruling.

In *Mouth*, Gwin made sure to publish consumer information on how to demand enforcement, listing the telephone numbers of federal agencies. She assigned Jennifer Burnett to do a Q&A with a lawyer from the regional Department of Health and Human Services Office of Civil Rights. In the red accounting book, she recorded that the clearinghouse project, which included putting together a how-to binder, had become a "tidal wave" and likened it to the heavy workload that went into opening Hoosier Bill's. She also noted that she was desperate for money and "terrified." A lot of the work for the clearinghouse fell on *Mouth* staff, which was essentially Gwin, Olin, office manager Cal Grandy, and three reporters. Gwin received a mountain of mail in response to the notice of the new partnership. She and her staff assembled a station wagon load of "Jumpstart Kits," a binder of items she mailed to those who signed up for clearinghouse materials.

She celebrated the magazine's ten-year anniversary with a cover that showed a blind man holding a "Disabled and Proud" poster in a street demonstration. The July 2000 issue looked back at the previous decade with highlights of the magazine's work. She correctly anticipated the future by warning that she would probably keep getting into "horrendous financial straits for excellent causes."[4] After fighting since 1990, she also said New Medico had gone down, but "I'm still working on that liberty thing."[5]

By the middle of 2000, Mary Johnson had discontinued working on the clearinghouse project, pleading too much work. Gwin kept it up and even waded into high technology, developing a crude website for *Mouth*. She also drummed up support for another ADAPT rally outside the Supreme Court to protect the ADA from an attempt by Alabama to diminish it.

In these warm months, Gwin would stick her feet in the goldfish pond to relieve stress. She recorded the deaths of fish. Work filled much of her days, and by the fall she had done something to deal with her loneliness. Three days before Halloween, she took in a hound dog from the pound. She named it Homegirl, though "Homey" was more of a rover and often tried to bust out of the fenced backyard.

Gwin herself became almost reclusive, a casually dressed homebody in clothes she picked up at the local Salvation Army store. She chased her dog and played with her ferrets. Her meals tended to come from a selection of Swanson frozen dinners. Siek visited sometimes and was impressed when she made salt potatoes, spuds boiled in heavily salted water, an upstate New York specialty. She hosted friends from the disability community in the new Mouth House from time to time. She looked forward to Mike Oxford and his young daughters stopping by.

Oxford saw Gwin as an asset to the movement and treated her as a family friend. Gwin excelled at writing how-to manuals for his organization and showed an artistic streak with graphics that came in handy for assignments. She also liked to draw and sketch for fun, particularly when his daughters came around. Oxford, who had suffered a serious brain injury as a boy, said Gwin was mercurial, but he understood such unpredictability. She had a soft side that many people did not see, he noted. In his words, she "adopted" his two kids. "She loved them and was kind to them, especially my oldest," who enjoyed drawing, Oxford said. Gwin stocked up on art supplies and brought them out when Oxford came by with his children. "She was artistic that way and she really encouraged them," he recalled. "She would get down on the floor with them and play with them and hang with them at eye level. She wanted to show her love; it was a very cool thing."[6]

37

In the first issue of 2001, Gwin published a twenty-four-page essay she'd been working on for many months. Featuring a black-and-white cover depicting Frankenstein's monster, the issue gave way to Gwin's research on freaks, mutants, sideshow acts, and other creatures from 2800 BC on. She wrote about the residents of lunatic asylums, survivors of chronic illnesses and accidents, bearded ladies, legless women, dwarfs, blind beggars, conjoined twins, and other people with irregular body types. The article, called "Building the Perfect Beast," asked a question Gwin posed more than once over the years: "What is normal?" Gleaned from a host of treatises, the essay called out those who label others. "That is bigotry and it does not belong to the Other," Gwin wrote. "Like otherness, it is in us all."[1] The article was Gwin's longest, and it served as the basis of a manuscript she later produced for a book she hoped to publish. In it she examined the issue of "normalcy." Its working title was "Monsters, Freaks, and History."

The Frankenstein issue drew a record amount of reader mail, most of it congratulatory. Gwin was almost satisfied. As she registered the praise, however, she also wondered why disability history appealed to readers more than the tough journalism she had published in 1998 in the Department of Justice exposé. "Colleen Wieck thinks it's because history gives us the idea we're much better off now," Gwin wrote in the next issue. "For the record, we're not." The item, part of her response to the mail, was preceded by a reader's letter telling Gwin: "You have a very clear voice which starts at 'edgy' and jumps up from there . . . [Y]our voice reflects the gravity of the struggle."[2]

Gwin often borrowed from comic books for graphics in the magazine, reprinting an illustration and putting her own messages in the word balloons. A series of three such covers from war comic books enclosed the spring and summer 2001 issues of *Mouth*. All three covers, in army green, featured cartoon soldiers in combat. "Boot Camp Part One: Basic Training for Monsters," "Boot Camp Part Two: Field Commander's Manual," and "Tactical Manual 1: Meeting an Enemy Offensive" provided guidance on how to fight the war against the enemies of people with disabilities by repulsing "compulsory normalcy" and acting "incurably oneself." She called for demanding one's rights, following one's own agenda, and rejecting conformity. "Every hero in history and legend has been an outcast," she wrote, "every heroic deed a monstrous deviation from the norm. Not one single hero has been normal, let alone *nice*. None of them fit in. Some have been crucified for their trouble."[3]

A remarkable essay in the combat series came in the third install-ment. The two-page piece roared like a battle cry from a sergeant in a war zone. It described what Gwin saw as the need for all people with disabilities to come together as a force and lauded the power of an ADAPT demon-stration. The essay was a call to action to the majority of the 54 million Americans with disabilities who weren't taking part in the revolution. Gwin wrote of encountering one of these persons during an ADAPT protest in the Washington, DC, area, probably the 1995 action outside the Maryland headquarters of the nursing home company Manor Care, Inc. This person, "Josephine Citizen," used a wheelchair and apparently worked inside the office building that the ADAPT demonstrators had surrounded. She wanted no part of the protest. Amid the clatter and chanting, the smell of urine, the landscape of twisted bodies, plastic tubes, pumps, leg bags, the humanity of Disability Nation, "Josephine" wanted to get into the blocked office building and hollered to security personnel that she was not one of the troublemakers: *"I'm not with them! I'm not with them!"*[4]

In a rare piece of video footage, Gwin reads the essay on YouTube. With a mild Midwest accent, holding a plastic cigarette holder in her right hand and with a fierce look, she delivers her "I'm not with them" line with utter disdain. "Josephine," it seemed, had personally offended her. Gwin was filmed in a short-sleeved plaid shirt open to reveal her "Not Dead Yet" dog tag (the opposite of a "Do Not Resuscitate" bracelet) hanging from her neck. She wears eyeglasses with dark round frames. Her sarcastic laugh punctuates passages highlighted by alliteration and her clever turns of phrase. At the end of the seven-and-a-half-minute reading, she seems to be near tears.[5]

She may have gotten choked up, recalled Jim Glozier, the videog-rapher. "Lucy was an emotionally charged person." He taped the reading at a hotel in Topeka in 2001, when he and his family were visiting from Washington, Pennsylvania, where he worked for Kathleen Kleinmann's independent living center.[6]

Glozier and his family were visiting Topeka because one of his sons, Kyle, who was featured in *Mouth* a few times, had been invited to

THIS BRAIN HAD A MOUTH

address the Kansas Independent Living Council's annual meeting. Born with cerebral palsy, Kyle was fifteen at the time. Using a power wheelchair and a communication device, he had built a reputation for speaking his mind about the unequal treatment of people with disabilities. Gwin was drawn to him and his two brothers, Glozier said. "She loved those kids to death." She would shower the boys with gifts from her inventory of items advertised in the back of *Mouth*, many of which she had developed and which showed her caustic sense of humor. Glozier's son Jason got into trouble for taking one such present to elementary school—a lunchbox covered with messages about syphilis warning signs. Jason went on to become coordinator of the Madison, Wisconsin, mayor's disability rights program, and Kyle became an employee of Kleinmann's Washington, Pennsylvania, center for disability services.

PART FIVE

Don't let me die. I've got too much to do.
—*Huey Long*

38

On June 22, 2002, Justin Dart Jr. died at age seventy-one in Washington, DC. His legacy included decades of disability rights proselytizing after crisscrossing the country with his wife, Yoshiko, to listen to and learn from people with disabilities about their needs and problems. Gwin had written about him for years and had published his picture numerous times, usually from photos by Olin. Olin's black-and-white portrait of Dart was on the cover of *Mouth* number 73, the September–October 2002 issue. With his trademark Lone Star cowboy hat, eyeglasses sliding down his nose, and penetrating eyes, Dart stares directly at the viewer in the photo. He seems to be listening intently again. The magazine was full of Olin's images of Dart—sitting in his modest wheelchair amid demonstrators, behind the microphone at meetings, or side by side with Yoshiko. Gwin did not note the death in her accounting book but did mention in the margin "great reaction on #73."[1] Numerous tributes from magazine staffers and writers and others filled that issue.

Gwin wrote a story about the memorial service for Dart. It was conducted at the New York Avenue Presbyterian Church in Washington, DC. The church had hosted Abraham Lincoln for prayer, and Martin Luther King Jr. for preaching, and ADAPT leaders for training sessions. Dozens of people attended. The roster of speakers included former president Bill Clinton. Gwin watched on C-SPAN. As part of the tribute, Yoshiko Dart handed out copies of a brochure containing her husband's empowerment manifesto. It called for a revolution to create equality for all human beings. The brochure listed the names of leaders Dart called "magnificent" people who had counseled him and sacrificed for him. "Some of them are well known, many are not," he said about his "empowerment 249." He included Lincoln, King, and Bill and Hillary Clinton, as well as many individuals who had been featured in *Mouth*, such as ADAPT leaders Kathleen Kleinmann, Bob Kafka, and Stephanie Thomas. It also contained the names of Janine Bertram and Evan Kemp. And it included Gwin and Olin. In issue 73, Gwin quoted one of Dart's profundities: "Justin Dart's Rule Number one: 'Don't let the bastards get you down.'"[2]

The Darts had been regular supporters of Gwin, writing checks and sending notes of praise and encouragement. In one message, on August 27, 2001, they wrote: "We are proud of you. You play a unique role in our advocacy for justice. We are privileged to be associated with you in the struggle. We love you so much."[3] In still another letter not long before he died, Dart wrote about the need to protect the "Human Dream" of equality and lamented how it was under attack from powerful forces on the far right. He concluded, "I believe in Mouth as a powerful and necessary voice in the wilderness of democracy."[4]

In the wake of the 9/11 terrorist strikes in America, the Darts wrote to Gwin saying that the best way to honor the tragedy's dead and to defeat terrorism was to defeat the causes of terrorist acts—poverty, oppression, and violence. "You are doing that," he told Gwin. "We consider you and Mouth to be the leading public media voice for a culture of free enterprise democracy that will include all people." He enclosed a check for $250, which he said would be the first of a series in 2002. He also apologized for not being able to afford to send more because of his massive medical bills.[5] A little more than six months later, Dart was dead, but Yoshiko continued sending the checks. Besides the needed funds and emotional support, Gwin received something else of value from Dart: one of his cowboy hats, made for him by Texas Hatters.[6]

39

During *Mouth*'s eighteen-year run, humor cartoonists embellished its pages. No one contributed more cartoons than Scott H. Chambers. With a distinctive style—characters drawn with sharp features—and a cynical point of view, his images were as biting as the articles edited and written by Gwin. Any disability-related topic was fair game. His characters walk into traffic with a blind Boy Scout, pee into barrels for Red Cross urine drives, purchase medications from indifferent pharmacists, or receive incompetent services from therapists, counselors, and doctors. He drew one-legged tap dancers, seeing-eye dwarfs, and an amusement park where the able-bodied pay a dollar to go on the wheelchair ride.

Chambers said Gwin appreciated his dark jokes. "You have to be pretty far into the pain to see the humor in it," he noted. He mailed Gwin about ten cartoons a month from his California home. Gwin selected most but rejected a few, for instance, if she thought they were sexist, like one depicting a dumb response from a woman to a man's line. Gwin paid for what she published. The cartoonist never met Gwin, but they had a regular telephone relationship. "Her way to deal with that serious thing was to laugh very loudly over the phone," Chambers recalled. "I think it was therapy for her."[1]

Gwin published 750 Chambers cartoons in her magazine. That helped him launch his career, which grew to include more than 3,500 images in a variety of publications. *Mouth* was special, though, because it gave him a platform to be his most unfiltered, he said. Like Gwin, Chambers objected to Dr. Kevorkian and his kind. One of his cartoons depicted a physician assisting in a suicide by smothering someone with a pillow. In another, he drew "Young Kevorkian," which showed a bespectacled boy in short pants dropping Alka-Selzer into a goldfish bowl. Gwin liked it so much she used it in Not Dead Yet materials.

40

Even though Justin Dart Jr. had implored his survivors in the movement to refuse to let the bastards get them down, Gwin was finding it harder to laugh. She was tiring of constant money woes and difficulties getting her magazine prepared under print deadlines. As issue 81 was going to press in 2003, she gave vent to pessimism. "Picture it all just winding down forever, down down," she wrote in the red accounting book.[1] Her spirits picked up because of a visit from some of her friends. For a week she hosted the group, led by Roland "Rollo" Sykes, an outspoken activist who was featured in *Mouth*. The former coal miner, who was disabled from a mine accident in 1972, traveled around in a big bus dubbed the "Great White Cloud." Accompanying him were Kathleen Kleinmann, the ADAPT leader who ran the Washington, Pennsylvania, independent living center, and Teresa Torres, the executive director of Everybody Counts, a not-for-profit organization for people with disabilities in northwest Indiana. According to Torres, the visit was glorious, filled with deep conversation and laughs. "That was probably one of the best weeks of my life," she recalled nearly fifteen years later. Being a friend to Gwin could be a hassle, but it was worth it, she said, for the "rush" of interacting with her—"kind of like if you're eating really good food and all the taste buds light up. It's like what would happen with your mind having a conversation."[2]

A few years earlier, Gwin had tested the limits of the friendship. Gwin had met with Torres in her home in Merrillville, Indiana, not far from Chicago, and it was then that Torres felt the force of Gwin's volatility. While waiting for Kleinmann to pick her up to tour the Chicago Aquarium, Gwin chatted with Torres. They discussed the idea of freeing all nursing home residents en masse. Torres opined that it wouldn't be feasible, but Gwin disagreed. "I said, 'Where are we going to put them?'" recalled Torres. "She hauled off and busted me in the temple."

Kleinmann confirmed seeing the red mark on Torres's face and getting the story from both Gwin and Torres. "Teresa wouldn't concede and say Lucy was right," said Kleinmann, so Gwin had to strike her. It took a concerted effort by Sykes over time to get Torres, who was a member of the board of directors of Free Hand Press and a writer for the magazine, to resume her relationship with Gwin.[3]

Gwin's concerns soon shifted to her own need for nursing care after she became so sick she had to be hospitalized. In 2004 she had hired a handyman to work on a renovation project at her Topeka ranch home, including sanding a Formica counter. The dust generated filled the rooms. That exacerbated the poor condition of her lungs from years of smoking, according to several friends. By the end of the year, the Mouth House had become uninhabitable and she was barely able to breathe. In the January–February 2005 issue of Mouth, Gwin notified readers that she was off to the hospital that had already saved her life the previous winter. In the next issue she wrote that she had undergone surgery and was using a breathing machine for an hour a day. It would be the beginning of her reliance on oxygen tanks for much of the rest of her life. She became resigned to needing this "oxygen leash."

But she didn't complain. Instead she wrote that she was refocusing her energies on fighting the "right to die" movement. "Once again I hear that death train bearing down on us," she said. "We must stop that train."[4] Once the Mouth House was cleared of dust, she returned home to work, tend her goldfish, and frolic with her ferrets.

41

Among her obsessions at this time was a case involving a woman on life support who was much in the national news. Gwin's reporting on Terri Schiavo showed her unbridled passion for the preservation of life and protection of people with disabilities from euthanasia. Schiavo became an international focus and cause célèbre for the Not Dead Yet and the "right to die" camps. Courts, legislators, anti-abortion groups, Congress, Florida governor Jeb Bush, and even President George W. Bush weighed in on whether Schiavo should be unhooked from the machines that kept her alive. Indeed, feeding tubes were inserted and uninstalled several times before the woman died in March 2005. Gwin wrote an essay about Schiavo's situation. "Death is messy," she stated. "Life is messy, too. Our hands are never clean for long."[1]

Gwin cast Schiavo's husband in the most unflattering terms as he pursued legal authorization to cut off his wife's life support despite the opposing wishes of her parents. Bitter legal battles played out in courtrooms and government offices, and each upward or downward tick of Schiavo's health headlined the news. Her story began when the twenty-six-year-old Schiavo, who had lost dozens of pounds through diet programs, fell into a coma in 1990 in St. Petersburg, Florida. A year later, doctors declared her to be in an irreversible persistent vegetative state. Her husband claimed that although she could breathe on her own, she would not want to be kept alive in such a condition, a view that clashed with her mother's and father's. After Schiavo's parents lost a challenge in a Florida court, Gwin called for readers to cry foul. "We must howl now or forever hold our peace," she wrote. "Howl before they come for you."[2]

The tug-of-war over Schiavo's life spanned fifteen years before her husband's position won the day. She was disconnected from her feeding device on March 18, 2005, and died on March 31. Gwin's blank accounting book reveals how despondent she had grown over the Schiavo case. Her record keeping suffered, and she had even stopped work on one of her long-term writing projects. Across an otherwise empty page, she scrawled in the red book: "They killed Terri Schiavo. I stopped giving a shit and did home improvements instead of the books. (These books and my books)."[3]

Yet the magazine kept coming out, with the help of others such as Cal Grandy, her office manager. As Gwin grew to rely on others, she saw less and less of Mike Oxford. He was busy with ADAPT leadership, his independent living center management, and his family. She missed the interactions and became closer to Kleinmann, who visited from Pennsylvania to buoy her spirits. But Gwin fell into bouts of depression. She resumed writing about death trains. In autobiographical columns in *Mouth*, she recalled learning to read by sounding out postwar newspaper accounts about the Holocaust. "Little Lucy, age 2 and 3 and 4 and 5, said to herself, 'If *I'd* had been there, *I* would have stopped those bad Nazis,'" she wrote.[4]

Her poor health extended into 2006. She was sick every few weeks. "The worst year ever!" she wrote in her red book, but she barely kept records anymore.[5] The first edition of the year came out as a double issue, covering January through April. The editor's column was written by a fill-in, Phil Calkins, a former academic and retired EEOC official. A double amputee as a result of a fire, and suffering from multiple health problems, he barely recalled his output for *Mouth* when contacted in 2019 a few months before he died. He remembered Gwin as inspiring, funny, and an important builder in the disability movement. In the combined *Mouth* numbers 93 and 94 which he helped edit, he announced that ten people—including himself, Janine Bertram Kemp, and Yoshiko Dart—were matching donations dollar for dollar up to the first $2,360 to help the magazine through lean times. He added that a group of donors had given *Mouth* permission to make monthly deductions from their credit cards. The issue included pages of photos by Olin documenting the movement's marches, arrests, and protests. Olin and Bertram Kemp combined on covering a story about an ADAPT action in Tennessee, which *Mouth* called the worst state in America for its warehousing of people with disabilities.

In the same issue Gwin published a three-page essay about her recovery from the Formica sanding episode and her reliance on oxygen tanks of various sizes, including a twenty-pounder that traveled on a dolly. She had a permanent disability and it dawned on her that "this is my *life*, and the end of it looms large." She painted a gloomy outlook, noting that "when you get damaged, everybody's stories end in '*she died.*'"[6]

She republished a self-portrait, a drawing that had appeared in the magazine fifteen years earlier. It showed a frazzled abstract woman. "The word 'stress' doesn't begin to describe it," Gwin wrote in the combined edition that comprised issues 97 and 98.[7] She credited Sykes and Kleinmann with helping a great deal while she searched for a new editor. Gwin tried to recruit Torres or Josie Byzek to take over her duties, stipulating that the no-ad policy was not negotiable. Both women declined. "She lived primarily on donations, and not everybody could live the way she did," said Torres.[8] Byzek was in a happy relationship and had a good job editing her own magazine. She, too, opted for the status quo.[9] Gwin turned to Deidre Hammon, the woman who had fought for her daughter in Nevada. Hammon said she would have "love[d] to do it, but you would have to devote all your time to it like Lucy did."[10] It was up to Gwin to continue producing *Mouth* or let it die. She kept it alive.

But her business relationship and friendship with Oxford was fraying. "I was getting busier and busier with work, was active with ADAPT," he recalled. "I didn't have time." In retrospect, he said, he should have realized how much Gwin relied on his companionship. "I wasn't bright enough to see that me and my family were not there, her people," he said. Gwin, who often was downcast around her birthday, noted in January 2007 in her accounting book, "No hope or even interest," adding, "Whew. If it weren't for Rollo, and Kathleen and Teresa." It took her until February to start managing her weight and her "leash," she noted, but she wasn't in need of as much tank oxygen as before. She started planning improvements to her backyard pond.[11] She loved playing with the fish and letting them nibble on the dead skin on her toes. Torres said she got a call one day from Gwin complaining that something was moving in her eyes and that eye doctors were unable to figure out the problem. She discussed the situation with a veterinarian, who told her that the fish at her feet had carried a parasite that made its way to her tear ducts.

42

In 2007 Gwin arranged another move, this time to Washington, Pennsylvania, so that she could reside near Kleinmann and her independent living center thirty miles south of Pittsburgh. Kleinmann found a suite for Gwin in the same apartment building where she lived, which was almost across the street from the Tri-County Partnership for Independent Living. Kleinmann helped found the center in 1990, and it had grown into one of the biggest in the state. Gwin was a fan of TRPIL and of Kleinmann. Kleinmann awarded her contracts for writing, editing, and design services, and the center helped pay for updating Gwin's apartment. Both women were on upper floors of the building, known as the George Washington Hotel. Right across from the county courthouse, the hotel offered spacious and ornate first-floor lobbies and an elevator wide enough to accommodate Kleinmann's wheelchair and Gwin's oxygen tank. Moving back east was "more of a return from exile," Gwin wrote that fall in *Mouth*.[1]

That September–October issue covered many familiar subjects, including an ADAPT protest, but featured an extraordinarily long essay, sixteen pages, by Barry Corbet, a nursing home resident in Colorado. Corbet described his sense of imprisonment in the "ghettos" that housed people with disabilities. Running three years after Corbet's death from cancer, the article was reprinted from a version that appeared in an AARP magazine. Corbet had been an avid outdoorsman who had become a paraplegic in a helicopter accident. He was the editor of *New Mobility* from 1991 to 2000. His was a compelling personal essay, but its use was an example of Gwin's move toward filling the news hole with long vintage pieces, often about people who were deceased. She also continued to miss deadlines and was increasingly forced to combine issues.

In the next *Mouth,* a double issue whose theme was "Moving," Gwin wrote about settling into her seventh-floor pad in the Washington Hotel. "Heaven," she called it. "I am home at last," she wrote. "I will never move again."[2] Gwin's landlord would have other plans.

She considered her ferrets essential members of her household and replaced any that went missing or died or came down with distemper. Among her roommates over the years were Tandy, Odo, Idi Amin, Batman, Wooly Bully, and Moose. Gwin lived with Wooly Bully, Idi, and Odo in Topeka, but had to give up Wooly Bully because he bit people and the other ferrets. She acquired Batman and Moose at the Petco in Washington, Pennsylvania. Cards from the pet company identified them as "companion animals."[3] One of the ferrets among the four that lived with her at the Washington Hotel appeared to have human attributes: it made eye contact and seemed to interpret human thoughts, Tom Olin recalled.[4]

The Washington Hotel's landlord tolerated most people but wasn't a fan of animals. The landlord took steps to evict Kleinmann because she had allowed a quadriplegic man with a service dog to use her apartment. Gwin wrote a letter defending Kleinmann and complaining of the landlord's treatment, noting that she herself had ferrets. "I said, 'Lucy, I don't think you should have done that,'" Kleinmann recalled. It wasn't long before Gwin faced a similar predicament.[5]

Kleinmann sued in federal court and was able to fend off her eviction, although her quadriplegic friend didn't have a lease, so he wasn't as fortunate. The confrontations gave Gwin material for her columns. She wrote about the beef in the November–February 2008 magazine, revealing that the man the landlord was trying to evict was *Mouth*'s news editor, Robert Milan, who was living in the hotel with Daisy, "the most talented service dog I've known."[6] She continued the saga in the next issue, claiming she was being targeted for raising questions about unwritten rules. The landlord notified Gwin that if she did not remove her ferrets from the apartment, she would be in violation of her ten-year lease and would face eviction too. Gwin chose to sue.

Kleinmann advised her to take her complaint to federal court because that was where ADA cases landed, but Gwin filed her action in the local court. She lost and was devastated. Just before the legal defeat, one of her four ferrets fell or jumped out of her apartment window. "She was near and dear to it," Kleinmann said. She thought Gwin was going to leap out the window too. She had been telling caregivers that she might. At the time "she was very nonverbal, not her bubbly self, not her angry self," Kleinmann recalled.

According to Kleinmann, Gwin's legal strategy was to get the court to recognize her ferrets as "service animals" though she had warned Gwin that such an argument would not win, even on appeal. Gwin became hostile toward Kleinmann when she refused to testify in court that she knew the ferrets as service animals. Instead, Kleinmann again urged Gwin to take the case to a US magistrate and sue under federal law. She reluctantly agreed.

In the 2009 filing for the case, Gwin sued the owners of the George Washington Hotel under the Fair Housing Act Amendments, which protect renters and potential home buyers from discriminatory practices.[7] Gwin's attorney, Robert Brenner, with Southwestern Pennsylvania Legal Services, maintained that Gwin was a person with a disability. He argued that she lived with physical impairments, specifically a seizure disorder, as a consequence of a head injury suffered in a car accident in 1989, when she was hit by an intoxicated driver. He added that she also had chronic obstructive pulmonary disease as a result of inhaling toxic particulate matter from the sanding of a Formica countertop in her home in 2005. She had sustained a knee injury in 2007. And on top of it all, she had been diagnosed with primary pulmonary hypertension. He told the court that his sixty-six-year-old client was unable to breathe without the use of oxygen tanks twenty-four hours a day. She could not move any distance without a motorized scooter or travel even short distances without a break.

Gwin, Brenner declared, needed the four ferrets, which assisted her through their "ability to alert her by instinctive awareness prior to a seizure." He contended that they had developed a pattern of physically contacting Gwin when she needed help. The suit concluded that the animals helped reduce the onset and severity of the seizures, because once Gwin was alerted, she would take her medication.

The lawyer also informed the court that substantial funds had been invested in the apartment prior to Gwin's occupying it in October 2007 to make it suitable for a person with a disability; $40,000 of that was spent by the Tri-County Partnership for Independent Living. He asserted that the hotel owners were retaliating against Gwin for her letter protesting the treatment of people with disabilities. She had filed complaints with the state Human Relations Commission and with the US Department of Housing and Urban Development. The landlord's agents, he claimed, had harassed her: they blew an air horn outside Gwin's apartment, turned off her water, refused to fix her oven, and began locking the front door of the hotel without giving her a key.

The hotel's lawyer argued that Gwin had testified in the county court trial that she had a Pennsylvania driver's license and had failed to tell the Department of Transportation about her seizure history. The hotel's owners also said that Gwin had been given a list of rules that specified pets were not allowed. Gwin responded that she had never received the document. A copy of Gwin's lease, signed by her, was entered into the record as an exhibit. It showed she had crossed out and edited several passages. In some cases she had circled misspelled words and jotted down the correct spelling. Elsewhere she'd written next to crossed-out passages that she refused to forfeit certain rights. "Tenant does not waive her legal or constitutional rights, ever," she handwrote in her distinctive cursive in the margin, adding her initials.

43

When Gwin first decided to sue her landlord, she contacted several attorneys, including one of the top disability rights lawyers in the nation, Stephen Gold. Gold had pursued cases for years in attempts to give persons with disabilities an alternative to institutional care. He was the legal muscle behind the *Olmstead* housing segregation case before the Supreme Court, and the similar *Helen L. v. Didario* case which preceded *Olmstead*. He had represented ADAPT and Not Dead Yet and had been featured in *Mouth* several times.

He took a call from Gwin one day. She told him about her predicament at the George Washington Hotel. "It was almost comical and serious," Gold recalled. "I asked her, 'Why do you have four ferrets?' She said: 'They each only work six hours a day.' It was so sensitive and funny, sensitive to the animals and funny because she already thought this thing through." The Philadelphia lawyer had handled numerous discrimination cases by then, several of which involved the right to have service animals. "This one took the cake," Gold said. He turned down the case and told her to expect to lose, even though he granted that the animals may have been supportive and that she needed support at that point in her life. Gwin was unhappy Gold wouldn't take the suit. In fact, "she was pissed off."[1]

Gwin wanted the case to be heard by a jury, Kleinmann said, recalling Gwin insisting, "My ferrets deserve their day in court!" Just before the lawsuit was to go to trial, however, the hotel and Gwin settled. Her new lawyer persuaded her to accept the resolution.[2] The settlement papers show that her side received $200,000, but it took until February 2012. The hotel claimed it was settling to avoid further expense, inconvenience, and distraction. Gwin had to agree not to join any demonstrations, sit-ins, civil disobedience, or protests, or to support any similar actions, against the defendants.[3] Gwin used her cut to buy a house in Washington, Pennsylvania.

As the litigation wound through the courts, Gwin published the final issues of *Mouth*. The penultimate edition came with some sharp Chambers cartoons and the first of what were supposed to be three installments of a John McKnight interview from 1995 about the importance of community in social services programs. It also reported the passing of Roland Sykes, one of Gwin's mentors and biggest boosters. In that March–April 2008 issue, Gwin divulged that Sykes had sent her a video of the Washington Hotel suite to entice her to move. She noted that Sykes had been working on a film about disability rights when cancer struck. She was trying to get a transcript of his work for the next edition. Gwin also opened up about the intensity of the eviction confrontation, calling her life "overdramatic" despite her pledge to lead a more moored existence. "No more heart-breaker boys, no more broken-down housemates, no more meds that made me sicker, and especially no more *landlords*," she wrote.[4]

The next issue would be the last. A makeup for missed issues, it logged in as numbers 107 through 109 for May–October 2008, eighteen years after the first copy of *This Brain Has a Mouth*. It didn't include the transcript of Sykes's video as teased earlier, but it did contain the second installment of the McKnight interview, a story on Sykes by Teresa Torres, and another jab at the Department of Justice by Gwin. She noted the pending retirement of John Wodatch, the DOJ "villain" of *Mouth* number 46. She labeled him an impediment to the ADA and to an important protection, Section 504 of the Rehabilitation Act of 1973, the law that prohibited entities receiving federal funds from barring any qualified handicapped person from participating in a program or activity. Activists had fought hard to get Section 504 implemented, including staging sit-ins at federal offices in numerous cities in 1977 that drew media coverage. Gwin chided the DOJ, writing that its enforcement remained anemic, despite the ADA being modeled on the Civil Rights Act of 1964, which had resulted from the protests of the 1950s and 1960s. It had been enforced immediately on its effective date. Why not the ADA? She also noted all the holes in the ADA, for instance, the fact that dogs and common domestic animals trained to do work or perform tasks were the only non-humans recognized under the law. "The DOJ points an especially scolding finger at monkeys and ferrets, both of which species are popular service/support animals," she wrote.[5]

The issue featured a celebration of the twenty-five-year anniversary of ADAPT with multiple photos by Tom Olin. The cover of that last issue showed Nadina LaSpina, an activist and organizer whose family had moved from Sicily to New York City in search of a cure for her polio-weakened legs. She had interacted with Olin and Gwin over the years, particularly on the Not Dead Yet campaigns. Inside, Gwin displayed sixteen pages of ADAPT photos. Pulled from deep in Olin's catalog, they featured Mike Oxford, Stephanie Thomas, Sykes, Dawn Russell, and Bob Kafka. They chronicled demonstrations and marches, people chanting open-mouthed, ADAPT followers smiling and protesting and holding signs with messages such as "Stop Funding Institutions." Gwin wrote a lead-in to the photo essay saying that ADAPT, "no matter its imperfections, has borne our truths, our demands, shouting out loud for all of us these twenty-five years."[6]

Gwin and *Mouth* were low on funds that fall, and in that issue, number 109, she appealed for "heroes" to donate so that there would be an issue 110. "We've had hard times, harder times, and times when I wept alone in public places over the real and final bitter end," she told her readers.[7] She promoted the next issue. It would be a "salute to disability's finest writer," Harriet McBryde Johnson, who had died in June 2008. "I explicitly told her not to die, and she promised to try," Gwin wrote.[8]

McKnight received the magazine and kept waiting for the next installment of his interview to appear. He was never told that the end had come. He assumed Gwin had become too ill to carry on. "She was the chronicler of a movement that almost nobody else wrote about," said McKnight, "and historically, if you wanted to write anything about the progressive end of the era, you would start with her."[9]

Eight years after writing about her Down syndrome, Eleanor Bailey appears in the final issue in a graduation gown, smiling.

44

Gwin got so sick after her move from the Washington Hotel that she had to be hospitalized. Cal Grandy, her office manager, still working from Topeka, confided to Yoshiko Dart in a note in early 2009, "Lucy is very unwell and convinced she's at death's door. She won't tell me why/what it is."[1] A home care worker who was devoted to her, Deb Crouse, who had helped her at the hotel and followed her to the new residence, saw that Gwin's energy was flagging. The hospital couldn't keep her. "They wanted to send her to a nursing home," Crouse recalled. "You know how that went over: 'I'm not going to any nursing home!' She was cantankerous." Working with Kleinmann, whom Gwin wasn't getting along with at the time, Crouse arranged attendant care.[2]

In late September 2014, Tom Olin was driving a bus around the nation emblazoned with "Road to Freedom," calling attention to the movement in a year-long "legacy tour" to promote the upcoming twenty-fifth anniversary of the signing of the Americans with Disabilities Act. When Pennsylvania appeared on the schedule, he made it a point to look up Gwin. Kleinmann had advised him that Gwin was unwell and urged him to stop and see her.

The visit was fun. Gwin greeted her old friend with a big smile. She was upbeat, happy to reminisce, and eager to catch up on some of the people they had known and worked with together. "We talked about some of our big wins or big adventures, like Not Dead Yet stuff, the You Choose thing," Olin recalled.[3] He was accompanied by a couple of friends, including his tour partner, longtime activist Robin Stephens. Despite decades in the movement, she was excited to be in Gwin's presence. She posted on Facebook: "Guess who we visited today? Lucy Gwin! Talk about legacy."[4]

A few weeks later, when the legacy tour reached the West Coast, Olin got word that Gwin had died. The date was October 30, 2014, the eve of the twenty-six-year anniversary of her rape in Louisiana. Not long after Olin pulled out of town, her breathing had worsened and she entered hospice care. She was pronounced dead at Washington Hospital. She was seventy-one.

About a year before Gwin's death, Kleinmann had visited her in that hospital, hoping to mend the break created over her refusal to testify in Gwin's service animal case. Gwin wouldn't let go of her grudge. "I was disloyal," Kleinmann said. Gwin said things to Kleinmann that still stung six years later. Kleinmann knew that the University of Massachusetts had contacted Gwin for her papers and that Gwin wanted to give them to the public archives for posterity. "She had great relief with that," Kleinmann said.[5] Gwin did not write much in her final months. But she left a great deal of material, including letters and manuscripts, much of it retrieved by Robert Cox, head of special collections for the UMass archives. Nevertheless, much was left behind and kept by Kleinmann, separately from the UMass collection. It was up to Kleinmann to liquidate Gwin's assets. She assumed executor duties because Gwin had alienated the people designated in her will.[6]

Russell Henry, the husband of the specified executor and himself the alternate executor, confirmed that he and his wife had become estranged from Gwin and left it to Kleinmann to handle Gwin's affairs. The disagreements had piled up after Gwin wrote her will in April 2009. She had fallen while still living in the hotel and had become unhooked from her respirator for perhaps a day or two, said Henry, whose wife, Susan, was a personal care assistant to Gwin at the time. He thinks that Gwin deteriorated mentally as a result of the lack of oxygen. Her mood swings became more severe. "After she was in the hospital after the fall, we went in and cleaned that whole apartment, top to bottom," Henry recalled. The couple babysat for the ferrets after smuggling them out of the hotel, housing the animals for several weeks on their sun porch. "They destroyed it," said Henry. "They were the mustiest-smelling things you ever saw." He added, "Those ferrets had a lot to do with the misunderstanding with my wife." All the same, he remembered doing odd jobs for Gwin and having some good times with her.[7]

Before her fall, she had celebrated the presidency of Barack Obama with friends. "Lucy had a big party when he was inaugurated," Henry said. About a half-dozen people attended. She laid out snacks. They listened to Obama's speech on TV.

45

Those who went to Gwin's home after she died found rooms filled with books, music CDs, and a big chair that smelled of her animals. Among the many boxes of things Gwin left behind and not collected for the UMass archives was a series of drafts of a partial manuscript she envisioned for a book on the history of society's notion of "normal." Graphics and photos of people she identified as freaks, monsters, morons, and maniacs populated its pages. It read like a thesis, with footnotes and citations, many referring to articles published in *Mouth* or written by some of its contributors. It included several Tom Olin photos and a Scott Chambers cartoon. The writing style was both conversational and scholarly, the work of years of study by Gwin, including a survey of the nineteenth-century thinker Francis Galton and his theories on eugenics and the idea of building better humans. The purpose of the book was to knock "normal" on its side and show it to be racist, sexist, ableist. She had mapped out nine chapters and planned a foreword by Nat Hentoff, the *Village Voice* columnist, who had been on her side in the Not Dead Yet fights and had written numerous pieces lamenting the death sentence imposed on Terri Schiavo. Hentoff, who died in 2017, had been the subject of an interview by Josie Byzek in the November–December 2000 *Mouth*, in which he mentioned Gwin's help in educating him about the disability movement.

Gwin planned to call the book *The Man Who Invented Normal*. She sent her manuscript to friends for feedback. It went through many drafts, the margins of which were filled with her handwriting and edits. In one draft from the fall of 2003, she noted that she had been born to nonbelieving parents and that she was nonreligious, "maybe irreligious." She modified that in another draft, dropping any reference to her parents and describing herself as a nonbeliever and a member of no organized or disorganized religion. In another, handwritten draft she had scribbled, "I am a full-blooded freak and I oughta charge admission for your secret thrill."[1] The theory of eugenics gave rise to methods for the selective breeding of people considered to be genetically superior. It also led to blocking procreation among those considered genetically inferior, as Nicholas Wright Gillham describes in his biography of Galton.[2] Eugenics led to forced sterilization in several countries, including in the United States, Canada, and Mexico, and wholesale use of the procedures in Nazi Germany. Monsters like Gwin would not find themselves on the right side of Galton's eugenics curve.

Included in her research library was a 1998 book, *A Morning's Work: Medical Photographs from the Burns Archive & Collection, 1843–1939*, with many pictures of people with birth defects, genetic diseases, missing limbs, or extra sexual organs. Gwin's copy of the book contained numerous passages that were underlined and marked up in yellow highlighter. "There is no treatment or cure for any of these diseases," one highlighted paragraph said. "Genetic counseling is vital."[3]

She pored over the words of Galton, writing notes on legal pads about her findings. Her hardbound copy of Gillham's *A Life of Sir Francis Galton: From African Exploration to the Birth of Eugenics* was full of sticky notes. Gwin's interest may have been triggered earlier in life. She wrote in a notebook that her mother had studied at Louisville Normal School, a teachers' college, and majored in eugenics. After graduating from the normal school, Verna Gwin became a special education teacher and, Lucy noted, advised "my sister and I to 'breed for brains.'"[4]

46

In May 2009, Gwin spelled out her wishes in a contract with a funeral home in Washington, Pennsylvania. She arranged for her remains to be cremated at a cost not to exceed $1,322, plus inflation. She wanted no obituary.[1] Kleinmann spread the word about Gwin's passing via social media. It took a couple of days for Kleinmann to track down Gwin's daughters. Christine showed up in Washington after the cremation. Kleinmann had laid out numerous boxes of personal items, photographs, and sketches. Christine looked through the material, assembled a few items in one box, and left after ninety minutes. She collected Gwin's ashes and went back to Illinois. "She was very nice," Kleinmann said. Christine thanked her for unwinding the estate. "Her expectations were not high. It was just closure is what she was communicating."[2]

Kleinmann had to figure out what to do with Gwin's assets—the secondhand furniture, a few antiques, piles of books, stacks of comics and CDs, a desktop computer, a laptop, Rolodexes, files, and papers—in the house and garage. She donated Gwin's clothing to people getting out of nursing homes. Gwin's big easy chair reminded survivors of her animals, and no one wanted it. Some things went to the landfill. Much of it went into the storage warehouse of the independent living center; Kleinmann didn't feel right tossing it. Deb Crouse, the former home care attendant, found a home for the ferrets at a rescue service and handed them off in a bag at an Olive Garden parking lot. Crouse had met Christine, too. "She looked like Lucy. I was in awe," Crouse remembered. "I said, 'She had her quirky ways, but your mother, she was a very, very special person to me. Lucy had my back.'"[3] The caregiver had become so trusted by Gwin that she had ended up on the board of Free Hand Press.

Tracy Hanes is close to her sister. They are private people, said Tracy, and Christine preferred to remain that way. Tracy recalled Christine's agreeing to go to Pennsylvania to sort through their mother's possessions and pick up some mementos, setting off on the mission at about the time their father was celebrating his fiftieth anniversary with his second wife in Illinois.[4] The newspaper announcement about the anniversary listed their five children, including Tracy and Christine, and eleven grandchildren.[5]

Hanes said she sometimes sees her mother in herself, like when she is under stress and gets a call from a telemarketer and lays into the stranger who disturbs her at home. She admitted this with a disarming laugh. She has experienced some bumps in her professional life for being too direct, and she wonders if that trait came from Gwin. "I try to rein in my directness," said Hanes. "Sometimes I'm not good at that." But her directness, she added, should not be taken for cruelty, as her mother's could. "She could be mean about it," Hanes observed.

She also pondered whether some of her mother's characteristics have entered the family gene pool. She has a son and a grandson, she said, who show elements of her mother. "Looking back, there's a trail," she noted. She has a smoker's throaty laugh after years of cigarettes. She recalled the Pall Malls in the red pack her mother used to smoke.

Gwin had been fretting about her physical and mental decline well before 2014. Upon returning home from the hospital in October 2006, she thanked Yoshiko Dart for a get-well letter and for Dart's continued donations to Free Hand Press. She said she wished she had another hundred years to work in the movement. "I will keep hope alive for as long as I do live. That's a promise," she wrote.[6]

During that time in the hospital in Topeka, Gwin thought about her mortality. She told Kleinmann in a letter that her breathing was so weak, doctors thought she might have cancer. She had been curled up, sleeping in a chair. In a dream, she wrote, she woke up feeling ill and called for her sister, Bridget. Gwin couldn't get her attention—she'd been dead thirty-eight years—but she knew that her sister would find her if she fell. Then she wrote about a true memory of walking with her sister on Wells Street in Chicago with a bunch of friends, including a boy Bridget had known and been best friends with since she was a teenager, perhaps Marc Thorman, the musician who was with Bridget when she took her own life. In the same dream, Bridget skipped and took Gwin's hand and said, "No matter what happens, you're somebody I can always walk with."[7]

Gwin said she wished she had hugged her sister that day. She wished she had told her she would always be her best friend. These were the things she dwelt on, she told Kleinmann, when "you think about dying all the time the way I have been thinking about dying all the time for a few years now." She didn't have any family anymore, which at one point seemed brave, as if it made her some sort of pioneering woman, but now she wished she had someone who remembered what it was like growing up a Gwin.

47

Gwin never made much money once she left corporate advertising. Her tax returns showed a woman who relied on her Social Security benefits. Those checks rose with the cost of living to $1,158 a month in 2014, or $13,896 a year. The year before her accident, 1988, she reported $40,968 in business income from her freelance ad work. In 1996, when she was running Free Hand Press, her income from wages and salary totaled $4,872. Free Hand Press's IRS statements were not reportable in the Form 990 documents that nonprofit organizations must make public, because the company did less than $50,000 a year in business. But some of the IRS statements in Gwin's accounting books show modest revenues, for instance, $6,692 in 1992. Gwin didn't get paid for editing the magazine. In 2004, while she was living in Topeka, her income reached $9,588. In 2010 she reported receiving $979 in wages from Free Hand Press. These were years when she was doing some consulting for the independent living centers as well.[1]

She had little in savings when she died, including an IRA worth about $6,000. She took out a bank loan for nearly $50,000 around the time she purchased her last home and listed her house as having a value of $70,000.[2] After she died, the Commonwealth of Pennsylvania placed a tax lien on the home to collect a judgment of $4,299 and began foreclosure actions to clear her debts.[3] Her Register of Wills file revealed the balances of her financial life. She had $87,213 in assets and $193,379 in liabilities. Her estate was valued at negative $119,623.[4]

Money had not been her motivation as a publisher. Eighteen years before her death, Gwin got into a running conversation with her counterpart at *Ragged Edge* magazine, Mary Johnson, about the impetus for *Mouth*. They began a back-and-forth in a telephone call in February 2000 in which Johnson gave Gwin feedback on her 1982 memoir. Gwin responded in an e-mail, firing off a screed that set Johnson back on her heels.[5] Looking back, Gwin acknowledged that she had failed to stick up for people other than herself. She felt she could have done more to organize and protect boat workers along the Louisiana coast so that they wouldn't suffer the discrimination and hostility she had endured. She wished she hadn't chickened out then and "missed the boat."

"I don't regret much," Gwin wrote. "I've fucked up way more often than most people, and I'm sorry about most of the fuckups, but don't regret them cuz I got where I was going or wanted to be or something." Now, she said, she was making sure not to shirk her responsibility to others. She was showing some courage, but this time in the disability rights movement. Gwin admitted that she was forever a fourth-grader at heart, believing in the Bill of Rights since elementary school. "What am I doing in the disability rights movement? That's an easy one and is probably obvious by now: I'm taking FULL advantage of my second chance," Gwin wrote.

She disclosed that she didn't appreciate something Johnson had said in their phone chat about Gwin seeming "crazy" in *Going Overboard*. She bristled at Johnson's use of the word "crazy." "Crazy? Like mentally ill? I don't believe you mean to say quite that, do you? Reckless, yes, I'm even proud of my lifelong record of recklessness. (How else you gonna have adventures, woman?) So I will own to that quality. And foolish, yes. If in believing that our Constitution means what it says I was foolish then I am a total goddam fool and will never retreat from that brand of foolishness."

She confessed to trying to redeem herself after her restaurant and parenting failures and pursuing what the psychiatrist Robert Jay Lifton called the importance of people changing their biographies when their lives take a turn. She said she had had a talent for single-mindedness all her life, and *Mouth* was an example of that.

Johnson responded with an apology in an e-mail with the subject line "regrets." She wrote a second apology three days later telling Gwin that she had risen at four a.m. to finish reading *Going Overboard* and said she should have completed the book before commenting about it initially. "You have lived more, done more, thought more, risked more than I ever have or ever will," Johnson wrote.

Gwin didn't necessarily accept Johnson's apologies, but she concluded: "If we can't figure out how to change the world for people with disabilities, I will take that Regret to my grave. Missing the boats. Wondering what I did wrong that we didn't get the battle for disability rights onto the front page of every paper every day."

48

Gwin had an ear for a snappy or poignant line and kept a file of quotes, perhaps for inspiration, or perhaps to use as fillers in *Mouth*. She corresponded with Leonard Roy Frank, a lecturer, author, and former psychiatric patent and staff member of *Madness Network News*. He had written a book on quotes, and she and Frank traded quotations they'd discovered.

The quotes Gwin collected herself ranged from perceptions penned by well-known thinkers and authors such as Albert Einstein, Frederick Douglass, Susan B. Anthony, and Mark Twain to those of friends who uttered something worth documenting. The latter group included Olin, Byzek, Oxford, and Maurer. She'd hold onto something she'd read or something she'd heard and jot down the line on yellow note paper and attribute the quote. She ripped pages from magazines and newspapers and underlined or circled something that caught her interest. On a page torn from the April 28, 2002, issue of the *New York Times Magazine*, Elvis Costello was interviewed about his latest album, *When I Was Cruel*. Author John Leland asked the singer what role anger played in his songwriting. Costello's response was highlighted with a yellow marker: "You don't become more reasonable—you become less reasonable."[1]

Most of the dozens of quotations filling Gwin's "Quotes" file are by others. But some sprang from her own brain. In her unmistakable handwriting, Gwin wrote a saying on a purple sticky note and stuck it on a piece of paper. It spoke of taking the course most would consider the wrong one: "The way to find the right way to go is by barking up all the wrong trees.—Lucy"[2]

EPILOGUE

Lucy Gwin was a writer who spoke like she wrote. You could hear her in the pages of her magazine. She wrote in simple sentences that exploded, sending birds into flight. She wrote about knowing how it felt to be trapped. She wrote about the prolonged fight for equality, the constant threats to the Americans with Disabilities Act.

She created statements about empowering people with disabilities and let her readers know they were not alone. Her magazine touched on the things her readers thought and felt and experienced. She brought attention to the dearth of job opportunities, housing, and training for them, the incompetence of professionals, the indifference of government administrators, the plague of isolation, and the vulnerability to prejudice and abuse. She hailed victories, promoted leaders, and praised courage. In the pages of *Mouth*, Gwin told stories about people taking on a society that misdiagnosed, disregarded, devalued, and dehumanized them. She wrote about herself, providing glimpses of what it is like to live with a disability. She wrote about disability pride. She tried to awaken people's minds to the possibility of gaining equality through unity. In the magazine's November–December 1995 edition, called "You Choose," she wrote: "We're tired of playing defense . . . Now it's our turn on the offense."[1]

Was her work significant? How does one measure any lasting effect of eighteen years of her advocacy journalism? Who will remember Gwin and *Mouth*?

In Pittsburgh on that spring day in 2019 when Tom Olin displayed his photo exhibit of scenes from the disability rights movement, Shona Eakin wheeled away after viewing the show. On the sidewalk outside the gallery, she talked about Gwin. A mother, wife, and head of an independent living center in western Pennsylvania, Eakin credited *Mouth* and Gwin for showing her a path in life as a woman with cerebral palsy. "It was critical to my learning about independent living," said Eakin, then forty-nine. "When you start in the movement, it takes a little bit to understand it's bigger than you. I did not know there were people fighting for our rights across the country."[2]

Her own story of working in the field had begun with trauma about twenty-six years earlier. She was serving as a peer support provider and helping people get out of nursing homes. But on assignment one day, she was mistaken for a resident and locked in an institution herself. She discovered the anxiety of feeling trapped. It happened because she was unable to reach behind her manual wheelchair for her purse to get to her ID. Exit doors closed around her, and a nursing home attendant insisted she get in line for dinner. It took her two hours to clear up the misunderstanding. "That was scary," she recalled. "Once I got out, I drove away and cried. I decided to commit myself to disability advocacy. To this day, I keep my ID on my joystick."

She has emerged as a leader in her state, suing the city of Erie, Pennsylvania, to build thousands of curb ramps, pushing for Medicaid coverage for low-wage personal care attendants, participating in protests, and running a big center that provides skills training, peer counseling, advocacy services, and home care. Near the end of 2019, Kathleen Kleinmann retired from the independent living center in Washington, Pennsylvania. Eakin's Erie center merged with Kleinmann's, and Eakin now runs the entire network. It is called Voices for Independence.

Eakin had sought to befriend Gwin in Washington years earlier and visited Gwin during some of Gwin's hospital stays. "She was worried people wouldn't carry the torch," Eakin said. "I told her not to be worried. Her work would never be forgotten."

NOTES

FOREWORD

1   For a discussion of both of these organizations, and for the controversy and split in the NFB which are beyond the scope of this writing, see chapter 2 in Doris Zames Fleischer and Frieda Zames, *The Disability Rights Movement: From Charity to Confrontation* (Philadelphia: Temple University Press, 2001).
2   Watch the Oscar-nominated documentary *Crip Camp*, directed by James Lebrecht and Nicole Newnham (Rusted Spoke Productions, 2020).
3   See chapter 2 in Joseph Shapiro, *No Pity* (New York: Random House, 1993).
4   See https://www.disability.illinois.edu/history-disability-services-university-illinois.
5   For more about Fred Fay, see https://www.ncd.gov/newsroom/2011/082411.
6   Shapiro, *No Pity*, 127.
7   Nadina LaSpina, *Such a Pretty Girl: A Story of Struggle, Empowerment, and Disability Pride* (New York: New Village Press, 2019), chapter 20, "Crips Are Beautiful."
8   I believe he spoke these words in March 1987 while giving a long talk at a conference, "First Partners in Policymaking," in St. Paul, Minnesota.
9   Nadina LaSpina, "We Want to Live," *DIA Activist*, January 1997. https://disabilityculture.org/nadina/Articles/wanttolive.htm
10 See https://notdeadyet.org/.

PROLOGUE

1   Kate Blaker, interview with the author, April 11, 2019.

CHAPTER 1

1   Personal ad copy, undated, MS 822, ser. 2, box 6, folder 2, Lucy Gwin Papers, Special Collections & University Archives, University Libraries, UMass Amherst, hereafter cited as Gwin Papers.
2   Draft of proposed memoir, "Bang on the Head," 1990, box 3, folder 25, Gwin Papers.
3   Personal ad copy, undated, box 6, folder 3, Gwin Papers.
4   Proposed memoir, box 3, folder 24, 1990, Gwin Papers.
5   Rochester General Hospital records, box 6, folder 16, Gwin Papers.

CHAPTER 2

1   Rochester General Hospital discharge summary, June 22, 1989, box 6, folder 16, Gwin Papers.
2   Ibid.
3   Medical bills, box 5, folder 12, and box 6, folder 16, Gwin Papers.
4   Joseph Maurer, interview with the author, March 22, 2019, and box 6, folder 16, Gwin Papers.
5   Bruce Younger, interview with the author, December 12, 2018.
6   Proposed memoir material, March 23, 1990, box 5, folder 10, Gwin Papers.

7 Rochester General Hospital records, box 6, folder 16, Gwin Papers.
8 Ibid.

CHAPTER 3
1 Proposed memoir, box 5, folder 10, Gwin Papers.
2 Ibid.
3 Ibid.
4 Ibid.
5 Frank, interview with the author, August 17, 2018. Frank's full name is not used by request.
6 Journal entry after accident, box 5, folder 3, Gwin Papers.
7 Ibid.

CHAPTER 4
1 Notes, box 3, folder 25, Gwin Papers.
2 Intent/mission statement, August 8, 1989, box 5, folder 29, Gwin Papers.
3 David Scates, interview with the author, March 12, 2019.

CHAPTER 5
1 Bruce Faw, interview with the author, July 10, 2019.
2 Keynote address, Sixth Annual Virginia Centers for Independent Living Training Conference, May 4, 1998, private collection.
3 Lex Frieden, interview with the author, February 26, 2020.
4 Faw interview.
5 Sam Baxter, interview with the author, February 20, 2021.
6 Justin Dart Jr. to Lucy Gwin, January 8, 2002, private collection of Yoshiko Dart.
7 *Mouth*, May–June 2003, 16.

CHAPTER 6
1 "I Used to Wonder Why Martin Luther King Junior Used Prostitutes," February 11, 1990, box 6, folder 7, Gwin Papers.
2 Paul Britton, interview with the author, August 9, 2018.
3 William G. Bauer, Woods, Oviatt, Gilman, Sturman & Clarke, Rochester, NY, to Lucy Gwin, February 13, 1992, box 5, folder 11, Gwin Papers.
4 FBI New Medico Health Care Systems, Inc., file, FBI Records: Freedom of Information/Privacy Acts, https://efoia.fbi.gov/#home.
5 Memo from Special Agent in Charge Thomas A. Hughes to employees, December 15, 1992, FBI New Medico file.
6 David Zimmerman, "Brain Injury Rehabs Under Fire," *PROBE*, December 1, 1991.
7 Ibid.

CHAPTER 7
1 Steven J. Schwartz, interview with the author, September 17, 2019.
2 Draft letter, A. Paul Britton to "Mr. Vertain" [Richard G. Vartain], US Department of Justice, May 6, 1992, box 5, folder 11, Gwin Papers.
3 Steven Syre, "Lynn Head Injury Chain Hit with Suit for Fraud," *Boston Herald*, April 3, 1992.

4   US House of Representatives, Subcommittee on Human Resources and Intergovernmental Relations, "Rehabilitation Facilities for People with Head Injuries" (February 19, 1992), 297–99.
5   Ibid., 43–45.
6   Ann Marie Atkins, interview with the author, November 19, 2019.
7   US House of Representatives, Committee on Government Operations, "Fraud and Abuse in the Head Injury Rehabilitation Industry" (October 29, 1992), 12.
8   Bruce Faw, interview with the author, July 10, 2019
9   US House of Representatives, Committee on Government Operations, "Fraud and Abuse in the Head Injury Rehabilitation Industry," 24.

CHAPTER 8
1   Mark Johnson, interview with the author, December 22, 2019.
2   Mouth, May–June 1992, 16–17.
3   Ibid.
4   Mouth, September–October 1992, 30–31.
5   Ibid., 5.

CHAPTER 9
1   Health and Hospital Corporation of Marion County, IN, Certificate of Birth, certificate no. 2271, vol. C-18, Marion County Records, 222.
2   Gwin essay, undated, private collection.
3   Lucy Gwin to Kathleen Kleinmann, e-mail, July 19, 2006.
4   Lucy Gwin, "Them and Us," Curio, March 31, 1998; and "Who We Are Not," New Mobility, November 1994, private collection.
5   Journal entry, November 1989, box 5, folder 5, Gwin Papers.
6   Fred Pelka interview with Lucy Gwin, transcript, August 25, 2005, Gwin Papers.
7   Photo caption, Indianapolis Star, March 14, 1954.
8   "Brown County 'Sage' to Have Exhibit," Indianapolis Star, May 19, 1957.
9   Lucy Gwin, Going Overboard: The Onliest Woman in the Offshore Oilfields (New York: Viking, 1982), 40.
10   Ibid., 196–97.
11   The Howe Tower, October 4, 1963, https://www.digitalindy.org/digital/collection/tchhs/id/13196/rec/20.
12   Becky Zander, "Girl Combines Artistic and Writing Abilities," Indianapolis Star, October 19, 1963.
13   "Herron Art School Honors 9 Students," Indianapolis Star, May 12, 1966.
14   Photo, Indianapolis Star, August 23, 1959.
15   Thomas Carr Howe High School yearbook, Hilltopper (1960), 117.
16   "Curriculum of an Overactive Vita," private collection.
17   Roger Marchal, interview with the author, January 24, 2019.

CHAPTER 10
1   "Tragedy list," November 11, 1989, Gwin Papers.
2   Robert Keller, interview with the author, May 22, 2019.
3   Marc Thorman, interview with the author, May 1, 2019.
4   Tracy Hanes, interview with the author, January 5, 2020.

5 Joseph Maurer, interview with the author, March 25, 2019.
6 "Tragedy list," November 11, 1989.
7 Chris Pulleyn, interview with the author, March 19, 2019.
8 Lee London, interview with the author, May 16, 2019.
9 Gwin CV, private collection.

CHAPTER 11

1 Fred Spears, interview with the author, March 30, 2019.
2 Photo caption, "Girl's Tragic Plunge from Old Town Pad, Round Up Hippie Pals," *Chicago American,* July 23, 1968.
3 "Cops Raid Hippie Pad after Woman's Plunge," *Chicago American,* July 23, 1968.
4 "Woman, 21, Dies; Fell 2 Stories in Old Town," *Chicago Tribune,* July 24, 1968.
5 Randy Sandke, interview with the author, May 1, 2019.
6 Gwin memoir materials, box 3, folder 25, Gwin Papers.
7 Marc Thorman, interview with the author, May 1, 2019.
8 Spears interview.
9 Sandke interview.

CHAPTER 12

1 Gwin writings, private collection.
2 Peter Walker, interview with the author, May 10, 2019.
3 Gwin writings, private collection.
4 Lucy Gwin to Peter Walker, October 3, 2004, private collection.
5 Gwin writings, private collection.
6 Rick Rogers, interview with the author, November 11, 2019.
7 Charles Vanover, interview with the author, July 20, 2020.

CHAPTER 13

1 Lee London, interview with the author, May 16, 2019.
2 Rick Rogers, interview with the author, November 11, 2019.
3 Tracy Hanes, interview with the author, January 5, 2020.
4 Lucy Gwin to Mark Holubar, February 23, 1989, box 5, folder 10, Gwin Papers.
5 Lucy Gwin, *Going Overboard: The Onliest Woman in the Offshore Oilfields* (New York: Viking, 1982), 11.
6 Michael Disend, interview with the author, June 12, 2019.

CHAPTER 14

1 Joseph Maurer, interview with the author, March 24, 2019; Lee London, interview with the author, May 16, 2019.
2 Chris Pulleyn, interview with the author, March 19, 2019.
3 Tracy Hanes, interview with the author, January 5, 2020.
4 Hoosier Bill's flyer, private collection.
5 Marjorie Lake, interview with the author, March 21, 2019.
6 Jackie Redrupp, "Measuring to Taste Is Her Cooking Secret," *Democrat and Chronicle* (Rochester), November 3, 1973.
7 William M. Thompson, interview with the author, June 2, 2020.
8 Lee London, interview with the author, May 16, 2019.

9   Susan Plunkett, interview with the author, January 15, 2019.
10 Nancy Fairless, interview with the author, March 11, 2019.
11 Hanes interview.

CHAPTER 15

1   Tin Rhino mailer, private collection.
2   Josh Schrei, interview with the author, December 2, 2019.
3   William M. Thompson, interview with the author, June 2, 2020.
4   Mark Seganish, interview with the author, January 9, 2020; Chris Pulleyn and David Scates, interviews with the author, January 2020.
5   Lucy Gwin to Joel Frank, May 3, 1990, box 4, folder 25, Gwin Papers.
6   Lucy Gwin, poem compositions, private collection.
7   Fred Spears, interview with the author, March 30, 2019.
8   Lucy Gwin, "The I Am Not Satisfied Book," private collection.
9   Joseph Maurer, interview with the author, March 25, 2019.

CHAPTER 16

1   Lucy Gwin, *Going Overboard: The Onliest Woman in the Offshore Oilfields* (New York: Viking, 1982), 12.
2   Joseph Maurer, interview with the author, April 13, 2019.
3   Lucy Gwin's U.S. Merchant Mariner ID, private collection.
4   Gwin, *Going Overboard*, 48–49.
5   Lucy Gwin to Chris Pulleyn, October 2, 1979, private collection of the author.
6   Gwin, *Going Overboard*, 220–22.
7   Lucy Gwin to "Seymour," January 17, 1976, private collection.
8   Gwin, *Going Overboard*, 16.

CHAPTER 17

1   Lucy Gwin, *Going Overboard: The Onliest Woman in the Offshore Oilfields* (New York: Viking, 1982), 9.
2   Tracy Hanes, interview with the author, January 5, 2020.
3   Gwin, *Going Overboard*, 260–61.
4   Ibid., 289.
5   Sue Dawson, interview with the author, June 11, 2019.
6   Lucy Gwin to Mary Johnson, e-mail, February 18, 2000, private collection.
7   Viking Press correspondence, box 5, folder 5, Gwin Papers.
8   Rhoda Schlamm, interview with the author, May 13, 2019.
9   Barbara Burn Dolensek, interview with the author, June 5, 2019.
10 Barbara Burn to Lucy Gwin, April 30, 1980, box 6, folder 41, Gwin Papers.
11 Barbara Burn to Lucy Gwin, November 6, 1980, box 6, folder 41, Gwin Papers.
12 Viking Penguin royalty statement, October 18, 1982, box 6, folder 41, Gwin Papers.
13 Carolyn See, "Obnoxious Lucy Joins the Rigrats," *Los Angeles Times,* July 6, 1982.

CHAPTER 18

1   "Today's TV Highlights," *Democrat and Chronicle* (Rochester), July 24 and 26, 1982.
2   Lucy Gwin to Mary Johnson, e-mail, February 18, 2000, private collection.
3   Kim Ode, "Lucy Overboard," *Rochester Times-Union,* February 1, 1982.

4 Stan Rogow, interview with the author, April 13, 2020.
5 Ode, "Lucy Overboard."
6 Margaret G. Maples, "Before the Mast with Lucy Gwin," *Adweek*. November 8, 1982.
7 Trudy Elins, interview with the author, June 25, 2020.

CHAPTER 19

1 David Arico, interview with the author, June 6, 2018.
2 "Edward Mordrake," 1980, box 5, folder 27, Gwin Papers.
3 Ibid.
4 Lucy Gwin, "Karen: I'm Lucky. I'm a Born Dyke," *New Women's Times,* February 1981.
5 Lucy Gwin, "Women Without Men," manuscript, private collection.
6 University of South Carolina, "Marriage Conspiracy," flyer, box 4, folder 43, Gwin Papers.
7 Lucy Gwin, "The Marriage Conspiracy," box 6, folder 25, Gwin Papers.
8 Lucy Gwin and John F. Foley, marriage certificate, April 25, 1983, Rochester, NY, private collection.
9 Joseph Maurer, interview with the author, March 22, 2019; Nancy Fairless, interview with the author, March 11, 2019.
10 Separation agreement, undated, box 5, folder 12, Gwin Papers.
11 Certificate of filing separation agreement, reference b1992/2765 200909240838, Clerk, Monroe County, NY, September 24, 2009.
12 Verna Gwin to Ethel Davis, June 2, 1983, box 4, folder 45, Gwin Papers.

CHAPTER 20

1 Lucy Gwin to Eric Mower "Himself," Eric Mower & Associates, Syracuse, NY, November 6, 1985, box 4, folder 16, Gwin Papers.
2 Lucy Gwin to Jim Morry, Hutchins Young & Rubicam, Rochester, NY, February 8, 1985, box 4, folder 16, Gwin Papers.
3 Emmett Michie, interview with the author, February 24, 2021; Bruce Younger, e-mail to the author, February 25, 2021.
4 "Rochester Business in Brief," *Democrat and Chronicle* (Rochester), July 4, 1988.
5 Robert Frick, "Agencies Call in Creative Hit Squad," *Democrat and Chronicle* (Rochester), August 29, 1986.
6 Michie interview.

CHAPTER 21

1 Sue Dawson, interview with the author, June 11, 2019.
2 Terri Tronstein Jerry, interview with the author, December 14, 2018.

CHAPTER 22

1 "Births," *Courier-Journal* (Louisville), April 21, 1939; "Gwin," *Courier-Journal* (Louisville), May 12, 1939.
2 Lucy Gwin, "Bang on the Head" manuscript, box 3, folder 24, Gwin Papers.
3 Notes, box 6, folder 10, Gwin Papers.
4 Fred Pelka, interview tape, August 25, 2005, Special Collections & University Archives, University Libraries, UMass Amherst.
5 Advertisement, *Indianapolis Star,* April 11, 1976.
6 Fred Spears, interview with the author, April 5, 2019.

7   Marc Thorman, interview with the author, March 1, 2019.
8   Tracy Hanes, interview with the author, January 5, 2020.
9   Lucy Gwin, draft of speech for Mid-Atlantic Conference, ca. 1993, private collection.
10 Pelka, interview tape.
11 Thorman interview; David Scates, interview with the author, March 28, 2019.
12 Journal, box 5, folder 3, Gwin Papers.
13 Lee London, interview with the author, May 16, 2019.
14 Fred Spears, interview with the author, November 5, 2019.
15 Verna Gwin to Lucy Gwin, birthday card, private collection.
16 Old calendars, box 5, folder 50, Gwin Papers.
17 Writings, private collection.
18 "Bang on the Head," March 1, 1990, box 3, folder 24, Gwin Papers.
19 Ibid.

CHAPTER 23
1   Journal entry, box 5, folder 5, Gwin Papers.
2   All quotes are from suicide note, box 6, folder 26, Gwin Papers.
3   "Bang on the Head," drafts and notes, box 3, folder 25, Gwin Papers.

CHAPTER 24
1   Ken Collins, interview with the author, November 11, 2019.
2   Correspondence, Lucy Gwin–Rhoda Schlamm, box 4, folder 31, Gwin Papers.

CHAPTER 25
1   Billy Golfus, interview with the author, June 7, 2018.
2   Journal, box 5, folder 2, Gwin Papers.
3   Colleen Wieck, interview with the author, June 11, 2018.
4   Sam Baxter, interview with the author, February 20, 2021.
5   Kevin Siek, interview with the author, April 18, 2019.

CHAPTER 26
1   Nancy R. Weiss, interview with the author, March 17, 2021.
2   Lucy Gwin, Minneapolis speech, undated, private collection.
3   Tom Olin, interview with the author, June 13, 2018.
4   Joe Ehman, interview with the author, May 15, 2019.
5   *Mouth*, May–June 1996, 27.
6   George Ebert, interview with the author, November 3, 2020.
7   Patricia Kolomic, interview with the author, December 29, 2020.
8   Josie Byzek, interview with the author, June 12, 2018.
9   Josie Byzek, "Shel Says," *Mouth*, May–June 1996, 9.
10 Josie Byzek, "What's Wrong with This Picture?," *Mouth*, January–February 2002, 17.
11 *Mouth*, May–June 2002, 37–38.
12 Kathleen Kleinmann, interview with the author, August 18, 2018.
13 Byzek interview.

CHAPTER 27
1   Lucy Gwin, "How It's S'pozed to Be," *Mouth*, July–August 1992, 23.
2   Lucy Gwin, "How to Live Longer," *Mouth*, May–August 2007, 26.

3 Stephanie Thomas, interview with the author, December 28, 2019.
4 All quotes are from Lucy Gwin, "ADAPT Goes to Washington—A Summary," *Mouth*, July–August 1995, 40–41.

CHAPTER 28

1 *Mouth*, November–December 1994, 29.
2 Tom Olin, photos, *Mouth*, July–August 1995, 31.
3 Fred Pelka, tapes, box OH5, and transcripts, box 11, Special Collections & University Archives, University Libraries, UMass Amherst.
4 Fred Pelka, interview with the author, June 14, 2018.
5 Lucy Gwin, *Mouth,* July–August 1995, 43.
6 Kathleen Kleinmann, interview with the author, August 18, 2018.
7 James Spall, interview with the author, May 17, 2019.
8 Vikki Stefans, interview with the author, May 2, 2019.
9 Deidre Hammon, interview with the author, June 27, 2019.
10 Deidre Hammon, "Speak Out? Make a Fuss?," *Mouth*, November–December 2003, 13.
11 Deidre Hammon, "The Wooster High French Fry Conspiracy," *Mouth*, May–June 2000, 36.
12 Hammon interview.

CHAPTER 29

1 Michael Bailey, interview with the author, June 18, 2019.
2 Eleanor Bailey, "Eleanor Helps Herself," *Mouth*, March–April 2000, 35.
3 Christine to Lucy Gwin, box 4, folder 18, Gwin Papers.
4 Peter Walker, interview with the author, May 10, 2019.
5 Tracy Hanes, interview with the author, January 5, 2020.
6 Lucy Douglas to Martha Christoff Spears, June 7, 1972, private collection.
7 Ibid.
8 Lucy Gwin to Chris Pulleyn, October 2, 1979, private collection.
9 Lucy Gwin to Christine, March 23, 1990, box 4, folder 35, Gwin Papers.
10 Lucy Gwin, letter to the editor, *Ragged Edge,* May–June 2000, 26.
11 Ibid.

CHAPTER 30

1 Lucy Gwin to Sharon Kutz-Mellem, August 13, 1991, box 6, folder 28, Gwin Papers.
2 Mike Oxford, interview with the author, October 7, 2018.
3 Mary Johnson, interview with the author, December 14, 2019.
4 Notes, November 1989, box 5, folder 5, Gwin Papers.
5 Sharon Kutz-Mellem, interview with the author, January 2, 2020.

CHAPTER 31

1 Lucy Gwin, speech, Virginia Centers for Independent Living training conference, May 4, 1998, private collection.
2 *Mouth*, September–October 1996, 47.
3 Lucy Gwin, curriculum vitae, January 1999, private collection.
4 *Madness Network News,* Winter 1983–84, 2, 3, 14.
5 *Mouth*, March–April 1991, 2.
6 Letter to the editor, *Utne Reader,* August 1996, private collection.
7 John McKnight, interview with the author, June 13, 2019.

8 Billy Golfus, "Care and Control," *Mouth,* May–June 1993, 6.
9 Justin Dart Jr., "The Reverend Wade Blank, 1940–1993," *Mouth,* May–June 1993, 2.
10 Bill Bolt, "Final Care, Final Control," *Mouth,* May–June 1993, 34.
11 Lucy Gwin, "The Hearts & Minds Project CD Version 2.0."

CHAPTER 32

1 Diane Coleman, interview with the author, July 30, 2018.
2 Joe Ehman, interview with the author, May 15, 2019.
3 Janine Bertram Kemp, interview with the author, September 18, 2018.
4 Lori Montgomery, "Outside the Courthouse, the Suicide Debate Is Less Legal, More Personal," *Philadelphia Inquirer,* January 9, 1997.
5 Lucy Gwin, "A Matter of Life and That Other Thing," *Mouth,* January–March 1997, 51.
6 Jennifer Burnett, interview with the author, January 18, 2020.
7 Gwin, "A Matter of Life and That Other Thing," 51.
8 Justin Dart Jr. to Lucy Gwin and Tom Olin, January 8, 1997, private collection.
9 Justin Dart Jr. to Lucy Gwin, January 12, 1997, private collection.

CHAPTER 33

1 Lucy Gwin, "A Matter of Life and That Other Thing," *Mouth,* January–March 1997, 50.
2 Clark Goodrich, interview with the author, January 13, 2020.
3 Free Hand Press accounts book, 1997, private collection.
4 Lucy Gwin, "Detour into the Death of a Romance," *Mouth,* September–October 1997, 46.
5 Lucy Gwin to Clark Goodrich, fax, fall 1997, private collection.
6 Clark Goodrich, "Wake-Up Calls," *Mouth,* January–February 1996, 29.

CHAPTER 34

1 John Wodatch, interview with the author, November 20, 2020.
2 Lucy Gwin, "Justice Comes Undone," *Curio,* Summer 1998, 27.
3 Sara Kaltenborn, interview with the author, January 15, 2020.

CHAPTER 35

1 Editor's column, *Mouth,* November–December 1998, 19.
2 Lucy Gwin to Justin Dart Jr., May 20, 1998, private collection.
3 "Keep Mouth Alive," June 1998, private collection.
4 Dana Washington, "Be Proud, Be Proud of Yourself," *Mouth,* July–August 2005, 10.

CHAPTER 36

1 Janine Bertram Kemp, interview with the author, September 18, 2018.
2 Free Hand Press accounts book, 1999, private collection.
3 Lucy Gwin, "The Reality," *Mouth,* March–April 1999, 27.
4 Lucy Gwin, "Lucy as Nun," *Mouth,* July 2000, 40.
5 Lucy Gwin, "In the Beginning," *Mouth,* July 2000, 17.
6 Mike Oxford, interview with the author, October 17, 2018.

CHAPTER 37

1 Lucy Gwin, "Building the Perfect Beast," *Mouth,* January–February 2001, 15.
2 "Incoming!!," *Mouth,* March 2001, 47.
3 Lucy Gwin, "Boot Camp for Monsters," *Mouth,* May–June 2001, 11.

4 Lucy Gwin, "Our Millions: I Met Them, in Person," *Mouth,* September–October 2001, 32.
5 "I'm Not with Them" read by Lucy Gwin, YouTube.com, https://www.youtube.com/watch?v=udZCMKZUDk8.
6 Jim Glozier, interview with the author, April 24, 2019.

CHAPTER 38
1 Free Hand Press accounts book, 2002, private collection.
2 "For Your Toolbox," *Mouth,* September–October 2002, 2.
3 Justin Dart Jr. and Yoshiko Dart to Lucy Gwin, August 27, 2001, private collection.
4 Justin Dart Jr., "What I Believe," private collection.
5 Justin Dart Jr. and Yoshiko Dart to Lucy Gwin, January 10, 2002, private collection.
6 Kathleen Kleinmann, interview with the author, August 18, 2018.

CHAPTER 39
1 Scott H. Chambers, interview with the author, May 15, 2019.

CHAPTER 40
1 Free Hand Press accounts book, 2003, private collection.
2 Teresa Torres, interview with the author, July 31, 2018.
3 Kathleen Kleinmann, interview with the author, August 18, 2018.
4 Lucy Gwin, "At the Mouth House," *Mouth,* March–April 2005, 28.

CHAPTER 41
1 Lucy Gwin, untitled essay, private collection.
2 Lucy Gwin, "Alternatives Depot," *Mouth,* March–April 2005, 5.
3 Free Hand Press accounts book, 2005, private collection.
4 Lucy Gwin, "At the Mouth House," *Mouth,* July–August 2005, 32.
5 Free Hand Press accounts book, 2006, private collection.
6 Lucy Gwin, "If I Were My Boss, I'd Fire Me," *Mouth,* January–April 2006, 55–56.
7 Lucy Gwin, "At the Mouth House," *Mouth,* September–November 2006, 48.
8 Teresa Torres, interview with the author, July 31, 2018.
9 Josie Byzek, interview with the author, October 9, 2018.
10 Deidre Hammon, interview with the author, June 27, 2019.
11 Free Hand Press accounts book, 2006, private collection.

CHAPTER 42
1 Lucy Gwin, "At the Mouth House," *Mouth,* September–October 2007, 32.
2 Lucy Gwin, "Moving to Heaven," *Mouth,* November 2007–February 2008, 28.
3 Lucy Gwin ferret folder, private collection.
4 Tom Olin, interview with the author, December 20, 2019.
5 Kathleen Kleinmann, interview with the author, August 18, 2018.
6 Gwin, "Moving to Heaven," 29.
7 For details of the lawsuit, see *Lucy Gwin v. Owner of the George Washington Hotel,* C.A. no. CV-09–00527, US District Court for the Western District of Pennsylvania, May, 5, 2009.

CHAPTER 43
1 Stephen F. Gold, interview with the author, January 15, 2020.
2 Kathleen Kleinmann, interview with the author, August 18, 2018.
3 Lawsuit settlement agreement, February 15, 2012, private collection.
4 Lucy Gwin, "At the Mouth House," *Mouth,* March–April 2008, 32.
5 Lucy Gwin, "One Man's Legacy of Destruction," *Mouth,* May–October 2008, 5.
6 Lucy Gwin, "A Shout Out to Adapt in Photos," *Mouth,* May–October 2008, 18.
7 Lucy Gwin, "At the Mouth House," *Mouth,* May–October 2008, 64.
8 Lucy Gwin, "Up Next," *Mouth,* May–October 2008, 2.
9 John McKnight, interview with the author, June 13, 2019.

CHAPTER 44
1 Cal Grandy to Yoshiko Dart, 2009, private collection.
2 Deb Crouse, interview with the author, February 3, 2019.
3 Tom Olin, interview with the author, March 3, 2019.
4 Robin Stephens, Facebook post, September 27, 2014.
5 Kathleen Kleinmann, interview with the author, August 18, 2018.
6 Last Will and Testament of Lucy Gwin, April 24, 2009, private collection.
7 Russell Henry, interview with the author, December 20, 2019.

CHAPTER 45
1 Lucy Gwin, "The Man Who Invented Normal," private collection.
2 Nicholas Wright Gillham, *A Life of Sir Francis Galton* (New York: Oxford University Press, 2001), 1.
3 Stanley B. Burns, *A Morning's Work: Medical Photographs from the Burns Archive & Collection, 1843–1939* ([Santa Fe]: Twin Palms Publishers, 1998), 74, notes on plates.
4 Lucy Gwin writings, private collection.

CHAPTER 46
1 Lucy Gwin, funeral and interment instructions, William G. Neal Funeral Homes, Washington, PA, May 9, 2009, private collection.
2 Kathleen Kleinmann, interview with the author, February 2, 2019.
3 Deb Crouse, interview with the author, February 3, 2019.
4 Tracy Hanes, interview with the author, January 5, 2020.
5 "Mr. and Mrs. Robert J. Keller," *Decatur (IL) Herald & Review,* November 12, 2014.
6 Lucy Gwin to Yoshiko Dart, October 19, 2006, private collection.
7 All quotations are from Lucy Gwin to Kathleen Kleinmann, July 19, 2006, private collection.

CHAPTER 47
1 Federal tax returns, financial records for Gwin and Free Hand Press, private collection.
2 Fannie Mae loan form, May 2010, private collection.
3 *Commonwealth of Pennsylvania v. Gwin,* state lien C-63-CV-2017–1999, US District Court for the Western District of Pennsylvania.
4 Registry of Wills, Washington County, PA, document 63-14-1344.

5   All quotations are from Lucy Gwin to Mary Johnson, e-mail, February 18 and 19, 2000, private collection; and Mary Johnson to Lucy Gwin, e-mail, February 19, 2000, private collection.

CHAPTER 48

1   Clipping, John Leland, "Sound and Fury," *New York Times Magazine*, April 28, 2002, private collection.
2   Lucy Gwin, "Quotes" folder, private collection.

EPILOGUE

1   Josie Byzek and Lucy Gwin, "Get Ready to Choose," *Mouth*, November–December 1995, 17.
2   Shona Eakin, interview with the author, April 11, 2019.

INDEX

INDEX

INDEX